HAWAII'S HOUSING "Solution"

"MOVE TO THE MAINLAND"

60 YEARS OF FAILURE
IT MUST END

PETER SAVIO

Copyright © 2024 by Peter Savio

All rights reserved.

No part of this publication may be reproduced, stored in a retrieval system, or transmitted in any form or by any means, electronic, mechanical, photocopying, recording, or otherwise, without written permission from the authors.

Table of Contents

Introduction 5

Chapter 1: Return to the American Dream 12

Chapter 2: What is the Problem? 25

Chapter 3: Demand 46

Chapter 4: Balancing Property Taxes So That Everyone Pays Their Fair Share 57

Chapter 5: More Tax Changes: Tax the REITs 63

Chapter 6: Hawaii was a Leader in the 60s 68

Chapter 7: Why Do We Buy Real Estate? 75

Chapter 8: Reducing the Cost of Living 80

Chapter 9: Photovoltaic Program 87

Chapter 10: Rental Projects 92

Chapter 11: New Zoning 98

Chapter 12: Hawaiian Homes 102

Chapter 13: Section 8 117

Chapter 14: Rental Buildings 122

Chapter 15: Rent to Build Equity 126

Chapter 16: What Would an Ownership Program Look Like in Hawaii? 129

Chapter 17: Legislative Action – A Complete Housing Program 139

Chapter 18: Changes in Government 151

Chapter 19: Send a Message to the Legislature 154

Chapter 20: Steps to Success 159

Acknowledgments ....**Error! Bookmark not defined.**

About the Author 172

Introduction

Whenever I give a speech on housing, I always start with an apology—because I may unintentionally offend someone based on how I explain the problem and offer the solution.

In this case, I am writing a book, so I must now make a second apology. I am <u>not a professional writer</u> by trade, but I find it imperative to share my observations and story. In the event that some grammatical and writing errors have proved elusive through the proofreading process and are still present, I remain confident ("knock on wood") that by the end of the read, a conversation will commence and a real path forward will emerge as we look for an understanding of our housing problem and the solution.

Before we continue forward, one additional word of warning: just like in speeches I have conducted, my written work is not intended to insult or offend anyone; instead, it is meant as a callout to ourselves and our political parties for our failure to question and challenge our own actions—for it is not any one person or group's fault. It is a community-wide failure.

We have all failed our community. I *do* mean all of us. Every resident, whether they're a homeowner or a renter. Our business community, our bankers, our labor unions, our news media, our reporters, our federal government, the military, and of course our political leadership at both the state and county levels.

We have all failed each other by not working together to solve the housing crisis. It is a crisis. So many people, including our families and friends, have left our state because of this crisis. For the Native Hawaiians, they have had to leave their homeland.

My grandfather was the general agent and owner of the Mutual of Omaha insurance agency in Hawaii. Mutual of Omaha had a weekly TV show in 1963 called *Wild Kingdom*. My grandfather sponsored the program closed each show with a statement saying, "Yesterday is history; tomorrow is a mystery." Basically, we live in the present; our potential in the present will become our history, and the decisions we make will write our future.

This is how we must all accept the failure of our housing policy. We thought what we were doing would work, but it failed. We need to stop making excuses for the past. Our history is written. What we did yesterday is already our history.

What we need to do—especially the Governor and our legislators, as well as the County Mayors and Councils—is accept the failure and find a new solution going forward. What we have done is done. Where we are is not your fault.

Your decisions in this coming legislature will tell us whether we have success or failure in creating affordable housing for our people.

We will decide our future and our community's future if we can come together for change and agree on a path forward.

I am hoping we will see that supply is not the problem, but demand is. The solution to our particular demand scenario is not building or increasing supply. Oddly, that may be the worst thing to do.

For 60 years, we listened to the experts. They were wrong. The lobbyists were wrong; the campaign contributors were wrong. Those who benefited from our present market did not want it to change or rock the boat. We have all suffered. Now we need to face the problem and find the solution.

All of our politicians should be judged by what they do to solve our housing crisis this coming legislature.

Let's live today and every day going forward to build a better Hawaii for our people.

Our political leadership does not understand real estate and is still trying to build out of the housing problem, assuming the problem is a lack of supply. Consultants and political action groups want their programs to be accepted as-is and base their program on supply as both the problem and the solution. Further, some want us to stay the course because they benefit from this present course. While this book is about Hawaii, I suspect many mainland states having the same problems will find that their government and the political party in control are making the same mistake. They don't solve the problem; they subsidize the solution. They do not look at the cost to us as taxpayers.

The politicians don't pay for their failure to solve the problem; we pay. Housing in Hawaii is a good example of this failure to find a solution.

One may safely presume that communities experiencing a housing crisis caused by unaffordable prices will have similar problems, as outlined in this book. I see three changes causing our increase in home prices:

1) A lot of the demand is due to wealth created by technological revolutions. This change created wealth and allowed people to work remotely.

2) World War II veterans using VA financing greatly contributed to the housing boom of the 1950s and 1960s, creating a huge amount of wealth. They have passed and their wealth has gone to their families. Their families are retiring and moving to communities with good weather.

3) "Airbnbs" have disrupted our housing market because the greater income that may be earned from vacation rentals has increased demand (and subsequently, the prices) due to potential returns. To some degree, the rest of the

nation is experiencing the same issues as Hawaii.

I am an affordable housing developer. This book contains ideas that should trigger people to consider alternative solutions to Hawaii's housing problem. It is not intended to be the "perfect" solution. This is my solution, but also a starting point from which a solution can be built.

A lot of the concepts mentioned have been used in my projects. We can solve our housing crisis by making a few changes in our understanding of its cause, which could point us toward the RIGHT solution.

Right now (and for the last 60 years), we have been doing the "same old, same old" and continue to fail at finding a solution to our housing crisis.

I am one of the few who believe we can solve our housing crisis in a 10- to 20-year period. To do that, we need to understand the problem and then build the solution. We do not have to destroy what we are doing now, even though it does not create affordable housing. We will continue with the present market, but make a few changes to support our affordable housing market. We then need to develop a dedicated and new affordable housing market.

We all need to agree on the problem and then build the solution. By working together, we can solve the problem and create a better life for our community.

This book contains my solution. You may agree or disagree, but that does not matter. All that matters is that we have failed, trying to build out of the crisis by building more homes for 60 years. We have failed miserably. To me, it is not a supply issue, but rather a demand issue. This book lays out my basis for the problem being a demand issue. The solution for a market distorted by demand is different from a supply problem. If it's supply, you build out of that crisis—but if it's demand, then building first is the worst thing you can do.

Please read and think of the solutions. More importantly, dream about how we can create a better life for all our residents, including those who have left.

With the RIGHT solution, we will house our residents at affordable prices and bring home those who have left our state because they could not afford to live in Hawaii.

1

Return to the American Dream

Return the American Dream, homeownership, to Hawaii. Undo 60 years of failure...

We elect politicians based on name recognition rather than what they believe—and more importantly, on what they say instead of what they do. Who has run for office with a clear program to identify why the cost of living is high and what the solution is? Who has run for office with a complete housing program (one that will work)? The answer is, none of their programs will work by themselves. They have vague promises of affordable housing, changing one or two aspects, but no one runs on substance. We need to be more demanding of our politicians and what they do. We need to hold them accountable. Trying is not good enough if change does not follow. We will (and can) solve our housing crisis if we demand a solution from our elected officials.

Milton Friedman said:

> *"One of the great mistakes is to judge policies and programs by their intentions rather than their results."*

An excellent description of the politics in Hawaii—great ideas poorly implemented. Instead of improving our lives, many of the projects and decisions politicians make increase our cost of living, essentially making it more difficult (if not impossible) to live in Hawaii. Our supply side housing solution is increasing demand and price, not reducing the price. Our present policy failed over 60 years ago. Yet we continue with a supply side "build more homes" solution.

Let's look at Hawaii today. We are in serious trouble. Our cost of living is running away from our local wage incomes. People cannot afford to live in Hawaii. We have a housing crisis. Rents are way up and unaffordable. Homeownership is almost impossible for anyone working here. The cost of both renting and homeownership is two-to-three times what the average wage earner in Hawaii can pay. To survive, residents need to have two-to-three jobs. Probably 60% of our families are one paycheck away from homelessness.

We have had these problems for over 60 years, and it gets worse and worse every year. We are now at a breaking point where so many families are forced to leave Hawaii. Our workforce is being depleted.

We're going to have to import laborers just to keep our economy running. Of course, this creates a whole new set of problems because we will still have to house the new workers.

Recently, we've seen 30,000–50,000 residents leave Hawaii each year. Hawaii has seen its population decline for the past 10 years. This loss is somewhat muted by the large number of people moving to Hawaii, who are mostly retirees and mainland buyers.

So, 50,000 people leave, 35,000 people will move in, and they'll tell you our population went down by 15,000. The reality is that in one year, 50,000 local residents will have left and been replaced by mainland and foreign retirees, investors, or remote workers.

The problem has become so chronic that there are now more Native Hawaiians on the mainland than in Hawaii. We are losing our people, and we are losing our local workforce.

HONOLULU Magazine recently had a quote on its cover dealing with housing, and I think it clearly outlines our problem:

> "Housing prices are up. Trust is down, culture and heritage feel threatened, and Lahaina broke our hearts. With record numbers leaving our state, what can we do to bring back our soul?"

I believe this quote clearly summarizes the impact and failure of our government to solve the cost of living and the price of rent and homeownership issues. This failure has hurt all of Hawaii.

It's important to understand that housing is at the root of many of our problems. It's created a lot of pressure on our residents. They want to stay in Hawaii, where they were born and raised. Their family and friends are here. They love Hawaii and want to stay, but their wages aren't high enough to pay rent or buy a home. Wages are not the problem—housing is just too expensive.

Higher wages will never get workers homeownership. The market has distorted so much, wages would have to triple just to have a chance to buy a home or apartment. Of course, if wages were to triple, the cost of everything would also increase (including housing), so it is not a solution, but a disaster. Unions need to support a housing solution similar to the one outlined in this book so that workers can buy based on their wages.

Parents and grandparents want their families to live and thrive in Hawaii, and it can be done. The proposed housing solution will accomplish that.

Buying a home is even more challenging, and nearly impossible for many of our residents. We are putting maximum pressure on our people just to survive living in Hawaii, which is destroying our community's soul. Our failure to find a solution creates many other problems such as alcoholism, drug addiction, divorce, suicide, crime, and physical abuse, among others.

They are all related to the unreasonable pressure we put on our people due to our failure to understand the housing crisis and our high cost of living. We need to find a solution to the twin issues: the exorbitant cost of housing and the cost of living.

I believe the high cost of living and the astronomical cost of renting and homeownership are all problems that can be solved. What we need are common sense solutions seasoned with a bit of innovation and creativity.

Our legislature has been working on the housing crisis for over 60 years and continually fails. We must understand why they fail and what is causing the problem.

To quote a well-known adage:

> *"Insanity is doing the same thing over and over again and expecting different results."*

This is absolutely fitting in our situation. Political actors may change with each cycle, but the same sets of strategies are repeatedly implemented—the "same old, same old." Unfortunately, politicians' attitudes about governance are often the problem. "Don't solve a problem;" instead, create a subsidy and then subsidize the problem so that the group stays dependent on the subsidy. We need to look for a new common sense solution to our government-caused housing crisis. It is a question of dependency vs. solutions and independence. It is finding a solution that helps the people. Government failures also contribute to our high cost of living and unaffordable housing.

Make no mistake, the government is the problem—although they would also be integral to the solution. You need politicians who are public servants, who care, and who are independent thinkers and do not simply follow the dictates of their party. We desperately need leaders who care about the people.

If we identify the problem, the solution becomes a lot easier to find. The purpose of this book is to offer an alternate point of view. Not necessarily to give definitive solutions, but to provide alternatives we can think about, discuss, and arrive at a solution the community supports.

Everything I present here is probably an oversimplification of what must be done. It may not be the best solution; some may say it is impossible to do, but the purpose is to get us as a community to consider a different path—to open a dialogue where we can all work to find a solution.

The solutions have to be thought through and structured to meet all legal requirements. We must find a practical but creative solution which, through discussions, we can refine and amend to meet the legal demands. This book is not the final plan, but the first step in the solution. It is the dream of what we can accomplish and plots a clear pathway for us to get there. I encourage you to keep an open mind.

When offering new suggestions, I've noticed that it's normal for people to say: (a) it won't work; or (b) we tried once before and failed; or (c) it's unconstitutional.

As to the first two points, assume there are no restrictions. Assume you have a blank sheet of paper and can create the perfect solution. Once you have done that, take your solutions and see how they fit in with all the rules and regulations. Maybe your solution is bulletproof, but it won't work because of laws prohibiting it. Never eliminate a solution because you think the law won't allow it. Maybe the law is what needs changing.

So again, don't be discouraged by criticism. This common sense approach should allow you to find the solution. The purpose is to force us all to consider other options; to believe there is a solution. Realize that we created this problem by not questioning what we are doing and not accepting that we are failing. We must believe we can be better; we must believe we can solve the problem, and we must believe we can make housing more affordable for local wage earners.

I know that a few years ago, a group of eight legislators voted against the proposed budget. To me, that was a sign that there were eight potential leaders in our government. This year, the bill to allow three homes on one lot was supposed to pass with overwhelming support, but it just passed by a few votes. I was told that my nine-page testimony against the bill had convinced a number of legislators to vote against the bill—an indication that we have a few leaders, and not just politicians.

Senator Brenton Awa, a Republican, introduced legislation to ban outside buyers. The legislature said it was unconstitutional and should not be considered. The correct response should have been:

> *"It is probably unconstitutional, but why does he think this change will help solve the problem? What does he see as the problem?"*

Maybe there was an alternative that would work. I am proposing that alternative. Our legislature and County Councils see it as a simple supply issue. Senator Awa identified a different cause for our housing crisis with a different solution: not a supply issue, but rather outside demand driving up prices. Senator Awa identified the problem, took the risk, and spoke up, but everyone was too quick to criticize him rather than ask WHY. Why does he think this will help? What is he trying to do?

It is imperative that we and our elected legislators remain curious. The question ought to have been asked, "Why would it make a difference?" We could have started the dialogue and gone down the road to understanding the alternatives that would lead us to a solution.

Senator Awa is a Republican, so he could ask the question, but being in the Republican Party, the Democratic Party won't even consider it. Yet the Democratic Party has been offered the same information. Still, the powers that be do not allow for a free flow of information and discussion. They have been told for years to try something new, but they wouldn't. The power behind the curtain (the "old boy network" or "insert-your-own-expression") doesn't allow for alternative views. You are not allowed to challenge or question the leadership. We are polite, but we are failing. Rather than work with the politicians, I am bringing the discussion to the public.

Also, I realize a lot of what I'm recommending are things we're presently doing or have done in our current affordable housing programs. I have done other things in my projects to make them more affordable.

I'm putting everything into one big pot, one big search for a solution, one big program with the sole purpose of structuring a solution that reduces the cost of living and housing.

Rather than saying it's unconstitutional or illegal and not considering or discussing all ideas or opinions, let's talk story. Then once we have an idea, let's find a way to make it work.

The term "unconstitutional" gets most people to stop and think, "Okay, that won't work." So, they don't consider it and go on to try something else. But remember, during COVID, you couldn't go to church, the barber/beautician, shopping, or even to the beach. You were restricted from flying to or from Hawaii. The list goes on and on. Yet most of those actions were unconstitutional by themselves but were rendered constitutional since a health emergency was declared.

So, realize that "constitutional" is not a black-or-white concept—it depends on the situation. The same is true for real estate. When the Mayor or Governor declares a housing emergency, they are setting the stage to do what is needed to solve the emergency—although we must be careful not to eliminate or reduce the cultural or environmental protections.

Don't be fooled by those who want to keep the status quo. A lot of people are benefiting from the present market; they don't want to rock the boat. Unfortunately, many of Hawaii's residents are suffering due to the high cost of housing and living, which is forcing them to leave their beloved island home and move to the mainland.

I am using what I consider to be a common sense approach to identifying the problem and then using common sense to find a solution that will work. So, let's go and look at the first issue—what IS the problem?

2

What is the Problem?

Commitment. It is a simple word, but not that easy to explain when it comes to building homes. Hawaii has a lot of isolated, affordable programs, but does not have one robust and complete program for housing that shows a commitment. What would such a commitment look like?

Our legislature agrees they are responsible for the problem and will solve it by developing a comprehensive, affordable housing program. We don't need a lot of independent programs—we need a uniform, well-thought-out program that will have our housing market speeding forward to satisfy our need for affordable housing.

They need to make the commitment to a complete housing program. If they don't make significant progress in their term, they need to resign.

Think of our housing market as an 18-wheeler speeding down the highway. Well, that is not what is happening. Hawaii's 18-wheeler has 18 flat tires. The Governor says "No worry, I am going to inflate the front left tire. We are going to build more rental units." Great program, but it won't work. The legislature passed a bill allowing three houses per residential lot—a program that shows no understanding of the market and will simply raise the cost of housing. So, they put air in a tire that has a hole in it, and thus it won't do anything but fail. The mayor also announces he is going to put air in the front right tire (new rental units being approved). Great program: it can be done, but it will not help solve the problem; it will only make it worse.

The reality is that they will fail because without putting air in all 18 tires, it is not a complete housing program. It is dealing with two parts of the housing crisis but missing the other 16 tires. So, we fill all the tires, but again, we will fail if we don't check under the hood and see that our engine is missing or "all bust up." Our engine (the government) does not have a full and practiced commitment to housing. So, we will never solve our housing crisis.

I believe the second problem is that we don't understand our real estate market well. Our leaders need to understand what creates value and how to manage our market. Hence, the benefits go to the local community rather than mainland or off-island investors and owners.

There is so much misinformation about our market, which has been distorted for over 60 years. We try and explain our market by using the distortion as a foundation, which results in misidentifying the problem. Then, we can't find a solution that will work.

With nothing to compare or explain the distortion, we cannot understand the problem. We can only build a solution on a solid foundation.

We are stuck in the distortion, not knowing why or how, or what is needed to exit onto a new path—a path to affordable housing. That is the real tragedy: we are stuck in our market distortion.

So, what is causing the distortion, and how do we isolate its effects?

Most studies on our market by government and private entities want to blame government regulations, shipping, and permit approval inefficiencies. Sure, they all contribute to the high cost of housing, but to a much smaller degree than assumed by our leaders.

This lack of common sense should make all of us question every government study, including studies by the UH and special interest groups dealing with housing, and especially those reports that consistently identify the problem as a supply problem. Most (if not all) of the private and government studies' conclusions are wrong. If they challenge their studies, they will realize why their numbers or facts may be correct, but the conclusion is wrong. All their studies do is create misinformation.

These 60 years of distortion have resulted in most people accepting that there is no solution to the problem and that housing is expensive and always will be expensive. They believe there is little that we or the government can do to solve the problem, except for maybe subsidizing housing.

Nothing could be further from the *truth*.

The most obvious problem is the belief of our legislature and elected officials that we have a supply problem. They therefore believe in building more housing to solve the problem.

They believe that by increasing the housing supply through building more, the housing price will come down.

It will not work for Hawaii's housing market because supply is not the problem. In fact, building more homes will make housing more expensive. We are only attracting more outside buyers who can afford to pay the higher price to live in Paradise.

We do not have a SUPPLY problem, but a DEMAND problem. Hawaii is a special place, and mainland buyers/investors and retirees want to move here. We are also attractive to remote workers. Being a popular tourist destination, we also have mainland investors who will do vacation rentals and Airbnb, all driving up prices.

Hawaii has gone from a LOCAL MARKET where wages determine home prices to a NATIONAL MARKET where prices are influenced by mainland buyers. In Hawaii, the market was mostly military housing allowances, Section 8 rental programs, and mainland buyers purchasing waterfront and high-end condos. This had minimal impact on home prices till the leasehold system was converted to fee simple in the 90s. This one change made Hawaii's leasehold market now acceptable to outside buyers as fee simple homes. Now, Hawaii is an INTERNATIONAL MARKET with buyers from around the world who can afford to pay a premium to own property in Paradise. Our prices are no longer tied to wages, as they would be in a standard local real estate market.

Our prices today are based on what the wealthiest buyer will pay. Prices are not tied to the incomes of workers in the community; they are tied to what an off-island buyer will pay.

Remember, a local real estate market should be tied to local wages.

Outside demand is so strong and wealthy outsiders have driven up our prices, making them unaffordable to local buyers. This demand gives those who are born and raised in Hawaii no choice but to move to the mainland. Our leaders' failure to see or understand demand is the problem. This is why their supply solution to build more houses and rental units will not work at making housing affordable.

Let's look at housing today. Homes are selling at $1,000,000 and over. Local workers cannot afford those prices. The first thing we need to do is determine what home prices would be in a local market without outside influences affecting prices. Doing that (while it sounds complex) is quite simple.

We need to disregard all the outside influences causing values in our market to distort. Those would be rental subsidies such as Section 8, military housing allowances, and federal employee housing allowances. We would also exclude retirees from out of state, foreign buyers, and all investors—especially those who buy rentals and rent them out to tourists or Airbnb. I would also ignore rental projects that are rented at above-market rates. Most people don't realize Section 8 rents are above market subsidies due to our high cost of housing, driving rent and cost of housing up for everyone.

The simplest way to put reality back into our market is to look at the definition of a local real estate market that is not influenced by the outside buyer.

> *"All real estate markets are local in nature. Homes will be built in that community and sold to people in that community based on the wages that are paid in that community."*

As per this definition, disregard all outside influence and only deal with local wage earners as our buyers. By definition, it becomes obvious that the price of homes should be tied to the wages paid in that community. In effect, it is a local market with no outside influence. We need to know what our base or target is.

Wages are local, and housing prices should be priced for the local market based on local wages.

Maui County recently conducted a housing study to answer the question of what was affordable for local Maui wage earners. The report came up with a value based on local wages (as of today) of $450,000 for a typical single-family home on the local market. For the local market, condos would be priced from $150,000 and up. By using local wages, we can automatically assume that no distortion is caused by outside influences.

The Maui study also said that a typical home should be selling to mainland and foreign buyers at $1,200,000 to $1,300,000.

That would indicate that the outside influence of mainland buyers and investors has increased Hawaii's cost by $750,000 to $850,000 per home. This simple test proves to us that it is not a supply problem. It is not a cost of shipping problem. It is also not a delay in zoning, approvals, cumbersome zoning laws, or environmental concerns, etc. It becomes evident that most of the increase is caused by the influence of outside buyers wanting to own property in Hawaii.

It is much more complex. Let's take a moment and examine the mechanics of how SUPPLY side solutions strategy results in the opposite objective of increasing housing affordability alongside the additional unintended outcome of making other costs rise.

Developers buy land to build, and maybe you can build 200 units. They then ask the city for a bonus to build 100 more affordable units, and the city agrees. But the unintended consequence is that the price of the land goes up, since more units can now be built. The next person to sell asks for a higher price, and the next buyer pays more to buy the land, but they don't need 100 extra units, but rather 150 extra units to make it work. I think you get the idea. The push for supply as the only solution is increasing land cost on all land.

But it gets worse because when land lease rents are renegotiated, they use the higher sales prices to establish land values. Consequently, land rent prices go up and those businesses pass the increase on as higher prices for their goods and services to us as consumers.

Higher value means higher taxes. Basically, we are on the political failure treadmill of rising cost of living and unaffordable housing cost.

Returning to the buyer market types, let's take a walk through them and how certain market buyer types contribute to costs.

Off-island buyers would probably be broken into two groups. The first batch is made up of investors who are buying homes and apartments to rent as Airbnb or vacation rentals. A house on the local market would rent for $2,000 to $5,000 per month, so Airbnb could easily generate income of $15,000 to $30,000 per month. Because the rental income is higher, they can afford to pay a higher acquisition price.

In trying to regulate vacation rentals, we are told that due to the high housing cost, we need vacation rentals. We are also told that they create jobs and tax revenue for the county and state. And while that may all be true, they also create hardship and burden for the local tenants who rent.

We are giving benefits to 30,000 investors, many of them off-islanders, sacrificing the success of the rest of our population for the benefit of these investor-owners.

Why let a small group of mostly outside investors succeed by sacrificing the ability of the rest of us to live comfortably and work in our home state? Our political leaders find it difficult to stop this abuse of our housing but constantly talk about doing everything they can to help make housing affordable.

Instead, they allow mainland investors to distort the market. Their idea of solving the housing affordability crisis is subsidizing housing with tax dollars, increasing our cost of living rather than solving the problem.

The second group of off-island buyers would be retirees/second home buyers. Retirees are important because they usually vote. They are welcome in Hawaii and contribute to our community. Still, they do not work and can afford to pay more for a home because the mainland was cheaper, and they could save more over their lifetime. Retirees also get favorable tax treatment. So, they may not be paying their appropriate share of taxes. We need programs to protect the local buyers.

The reason...

Locals have given up. Many do not register to vote, nor do they vote. The first step in the change to affordable housing is to get your family and friends to register to vote and then vote for change. You will make a difference. Get on the phone and the internet and tell them tonight to register and vote to join the housing revolution—we will revisit this further in Chapters 18 and 19.

It's important to remember that Hawaii is a small state with a relatively small population spread over the main islands. Outside buyers purchasing thousands of homes could easily distort our market. Mainland retirees have cash savings and retirement incomes. They can pay cash. They may have tax-free income. Hawaii's tax code favors retirees. Workers trying to buy their first home pay taxes, and our high cost of living makes it challenging to save the needed down payment.

By increasing supply to solve the housing problem, all we've done is authorize the building of more homes at prices that local people cannot afford to pay.

Look at the recent bill encouraging the building of three homes on each lot. Our leaders theorized that it would help reduce the cost of housing. It will not work. Converting residential lots into multifamily zoning will create more units, but not affordable units.

What it will do instead is increase the cost of the land. The homes will be built and sold at international market prices without connection to local wages. By approving the bill, the legislature created more value for the property owner but provided no solution on how it should be used to create affordable units.

If the law had required the units to be rented or sold at 100% of median income, then we may have a positive impact on our housing market because prices would be controlled based on local wages. Housing or units built under such a program would only be beneficial if they could only be rented and sold long-term to local residents. This is not rent control, but a second market specifically meant for affordable housing where rent increases are tied to wage increases. It is still a free market, but isolated from outside influences. A true local market. That simple change (renting and selling to affordable local buyers) would be effective. Instead, they passed what amounts to a monster home bill, but in three separate units.

In the new to-be-established local market, the government has no control. They only establish the market. Rents and prices are tied to wages in this new market. The big difference is that wealthy off-island buyers and investors cannot influence rent or prices in this local market. However, they could still buy in the international market, which remains intact under the housing solution I propose.

In current conditions, in the international market with the government-subsidized supply solution, even the "affordable" houses are out of reach of the local market. A number of "affordable" units have been on the market for long periods of time because no local buyer can afford the price.

Once affordable units became unaffordable, the government didn't reduce the price but increased the available pool from buyers earning 120% above the median wage to those with 140% of the median wage. Now, even buyers with 140% incomes can't afford to buy "affordable." With the current trajectory, they will have to raise it to include 175% of median wage earners. They are not solving the problem, but rather manipulating numbers to make it look like they are doing something. What they are doing is making housing more unaffordable and forcing us to leave Hawaii and move to the mainland.

Even now, our government is coming up with programs to subsidize the developer who is building "affordable housing" in our present international market. They put the unit on the market at $600,000, but affordable buyers only qualify for $450,000. So, we start with "affordable units" that are unaffordable based on Hawaii wages. The developer asks to put it up for rent but needs the government to subsidize it because no one can afford it at the market rate. In short, the affordable buyer could not afford to buy the house at the "subsidized selling price," so we are going to subsidize the rent so that the affordable buyer can live there. This program benefits the unit owner and does nothing for the renter or Hawaii's taxpayers; instead, it increases the cost of living, making it harder to stay in Hawaii. It is worse when you realize the $600,000 is for a studio or one-bedroom unit, while the $450,000 benchmark home is a three-bedroom home.

We are taking an affordable unit and letting the developer keep the unit and retain all the benefits. At the same time, the tenant gets none of the financial benefits of ownership. The taxpayer had to subsidize the rent but gave the benefits to the wealthy building owner. We increase our cost of living through this type of wasteful tax spending.

This is part of the problem. Politicians see housing as a place to live rather than a place to create wealth and, if done correctly, stabilize and eventually reduce the cost of living. If done correctly, we would create wealth for the tenant/owner-occupant and the community, not the developer or wealthy unit owner.

Instead of solving the problem, the government continually looks to subsidize the problem, which simply increases our cost of living and is destined to fail. By increasing supply, all we do is increase the demand from off-island buyers and foreign buyers. They will continue to purchase homes, using them as vacation rentals, second homes, or retirement homes. This demand is not caused by price, but by Hawaii's unique location, exceptional climate, and beautiful beaches. Let's face it: we're *Paradise*.

The demand from outside buyers will continue to drive our prices up. If our government was serious, they would control the vacation rentals in residential areas and buildings. They would look for ways to invite investors and retirees to come to Hawaii, but in such a way as not to distort the market and force our residents to leave. The government should control or have a program to regulate demand and then build an affordable supply in a market where prices are low and tied to local wages for all local buyers.

Please note that none of the proposed solutions champion supply. It is worth pointing out the mistakes our government has made in pushing for an increase in supply. Again, the most recent example was the legislature passing a law that allowed three homes to be built on one lot.

The whole purpose of this is to use existing lots to create affordable housing units that can be rented or sold. Allowing additional units in a lot increases the density and land value, so you actually end up making housing more expensive.

When you increase density in an open market, you increase value based on that market. A lot that allows for a single home has value. If two homes are allowed, the lot is even more valuable. If three homes are allowed, the value is even greater. A lot with one rental unit has value. A lot with two rental units has possibly twice as much value. A lot with three rental units could easily have three times as much value. Density (or the number or size of units that can be built) is what creates value in real estate.

Buyers will pay more for a lot where you can build two homes on it. This is true whether it is built for rent or for sale on the uncontrolled international market.

This same bill, if in the controlled market, would work since rent and price are tied to a market based on wages, not demand or supply. When the news story on the three homes on one lot bill made headlines, there was a picture in the article of a home built on a small lot. It was going to be typical of what they say the legislature would like to see built if this law were to pass.

What was interesting to note is that the house on the small lot was selling for $975,000. We now know that affordable is $450,000, so the homes they build will not be affordable. This law that Hawaii's politicians and political leadership pushed only changes our single-family residential zoning to a multifamily zoning. It increases density, triples traffic on our roads, strains our parks and schools, and creates the risk of wildfires. This allows cars to take all street parking, so visitors and families have no place to park. They are not making our lives better; they are making our lives more difficult.

Our leaders are making monster homes legal by allowing three homes instead of one monster home. We know how monster homes disrupt our communities, and that's why local residents objected and got monster homes banned. Our political leaders decided to let "no crisis go to waste" and use our housing crisis to circumvent what the residents of Hawaii want: affordable housing for our community. They tricked everyone into allowing three homes on one lot—the true new monster home bill. Let's hope your city council and the other island county councils reject it, or the legislature gets so many complaints that they repeal it.

Remember, an affordable house in Hawaii would be $450,000, so by adding two more homes to the present lot, our politicians are creating a more affordable home at $975,000, but for a local buyer, it is as unaffordable as a $1,200,000 home. The politicians are creating opportunities for the owner to make more money by selling three homes at what the market would pay.

Also note that Maui has allowed three homes per lot for years, and they have the worst housing market for local families. All the law did was increase the property's market value, which is sold to off-island buyers or retirees. It created no advantage or value for the local wage earner.

All they are doing is increasing the supply of units at prices and rents local families can't afford. They allowed more off-island buyers to come and displace local tenants and buyers. What our leadership is doing will not work, and is the worst thing you can do for the local workers.

If demand is the problem, anything you do to stimulate supply will probably worsen the problem. There is enough demand to buy everything that you can build and pay a price higher than what the local economy can justify.

So, demand is the problem. The solution, then, must be how to control demand to keep our units affordable.

DEMAND. That's what we'll discuss in our next chapter.

3

Demand

When demand is the problem, building is not the solution. What you need to do is establish a market that is restricted to local buyers being able to purchase homes based on their wages. This is basically what most states do with their limited supply of government affordable housing units.

We keep the existing international market for off-island and wealthy local buyers but do a better job of managing it, so it benefits the working-class local buyers.

The newly-established affordable market will only be for local families living and working in Hawaii.

It is not a regulated market but a government-established market that will operate freely based on wage increases instead of outside influences.

It is a free market; this would be Hawaii's market with no outside influence on prices.

Like a regular market, prices may fluctuate with interest rates, employment, demand, etc. The only difference is that outside buyers with wealth cannot drive the price of housing up, making it unaffordable for Hawaii's workers.

To establish such, the Governor and Mayors should declare a housing emergency. This will allow for more robust restrictions on wealthy buyers entering the new affordable market.

It is customary that affordable units are sold with restrictions. The restrictions placed on affordable housing by the government are being an owner-occupant, a local resident, 18 years of age or older, and a citizen of the United States.

There should be additional restrictions as to income and net worth. You would also expect some restriction on resale, where the property cannot be resold for a number of years.

Income and net worth restrictions are critical to stop wealthy off-island buyers from purchasing in the subsidized market for local residents. This may be easier to defend against constitutional challenges, as income and asset limits define the buyers who qualify for affordable housing. The concern restricting buyers to local owners could be a constitutional issue. Absolute restrictions could be a problem, but it is something that can be legislated around. For instance, being a resident and paying taxes in Hawaii for three years may be allowed rather than a blanket restriction on all off-island buyers.

As to resale, I would like to see a market structure where the resale price will be restricted for the life of the property, essentially forever.

This could be accomplished by simply requiring that all affordable buyers can resell at any time once entering the market. Still, you have to resell based on the wage increase and local market wages, rather than the open market prices. If wages double, the price of the home doubles. If you think about it, all we're doing is creating a market where local buyers compete with local buyers without the competition from off-island buyers entering the market and increasing prices to above what wage earners can afford.

Unions should support this type of market. They can push for higher wages, but their members' income cannot keep up with price increases caused by wealthy out-of-state and foreign buyers. This type of housing solution is the only possibility of getting workers into housing. Remember, you buy a house and lock in the cost of housing for 30 years. The loan is paid off, and the mortgage goes away. The union must see housing as granting wage stability, increased income, and reduced cost of living through homeownership. With normal wage increases combined with home-ownership, our people can live and thrive in Hawaii.

The only hope for the average worker (including union members) to live and thrive in our community is to support and demand a local housing market for local buyers.

How we select buyers eligible to enter the market is something we need to develop, but we already have a number of restrictions in our existing affordable housing market program.

All we are currently doing is structuring the rules based on the suitability of buyers. I prefer a scoring system similar to one used in government construction jobs. They ask factual questions, and the interviewees who attain a predetermined score get the job. I am sure there are other possibilities. It doesn't matter which system is used, as long as it is fair.

This is a rough suggestion of what could be done. I am not sure it is even doable, but I wanted to show the issues we need to look into at a minimum.

For instance, these are affordable restrictions presently in place. We only need to understand and elaborate on these requirements and clarify them:

The following is a hypothetical: POSSIBLE SCORE CARD USED TO GET INTO AFFORDABLE HOUSING GROUP ONE AND TWO. We shall structure it in the following ways regarding eligibility:

1) To get into the local market, the prospective participant shall need more than 50 points to be eligible.

2) To be in the second affordable buyers' market, participants need under 50 points but only get the opportunity if local buyers DO NOT buy.

We shall use the following as a scoring system to determine eligibility:

- Born in Hawaii = 10 points
- Educated in Hawaii, 1 point per year (max) 16 points
- File Hawaii State Tax Return, 1 point per year (max) 10 points
- Age:
  - 60yr + = 4 points, 50yr + = 3 points, 40yr + = 2 points, 30 yr + = 1 points
- Wages:
  - under 50% median income = 10 points
  - over 50% under 60% median income = 9 points
  - over 60% under 70% median income = 8 points
  - over 70% under 80% median income = 7 points
  - over 80% under 90% median income = 6 points
  - over 90% under 100% median income = 5 points
  - over 100% under 110% median income = 4 points
  - over 110% under 120% median income = 3 points
  - over 120% under 130% median income = 2 points
  - over 130% under 140% median income = 1 point

- Income Median for Family Size
  - Single = 10 points, Married = 15 points, Married with Children = 20 points
- Assets
  - under <200,000 in assets = 10 points
  - over 200,000 under 250,000 in assets = 5 points

*We may want to add a category where we award points for certain needed professions such as doctors, nurses, computer technicians etc. = 10 points.

Under this structure, local affordable buyers go into Basket #1. Hawaii taxpayers and residents get first choice.

Basket #2 is for buyers that have less than 50 points. They will only be offered units after local buyers in Basket #1 have had the opportunity to purchase.

We are creating a market for local residents, where wages dictate price. Whatever wages are being paid locally would establish the price and allow buyers to buy into the market.

Once a first-time buyer is in the market, they should be allowed to buy or sell their existing unit and move to a bigger or smaller unit as needed within the affordable market.

The first objection is that this program will reduce property appreciation. Yes, but the unit will probably be kept in the family and go to the children or next of kin over time. After all, the goal of this program is not appreciation, but rather staying, living, and thriving in Hawaii.

Also, appreciation is not the reason you buy a home, nor is it the greatest wealth creator. You buy a home to lock in your biggest part of the cost of living: housing. A mortgage payment could be seen as rent being set for 30 years with no increase. This allows you to keep all your pay raises over time, and then once the loan is paid off, you have a significantly reduced cost of living.

If the affordable market did not exist, they could not have purchased in Hawaii and could have only rented and struggled for a few years or moved away.

The affordable market gives them a chance to own a home—an opportunity to move into the free market or stay in the government-affordable market forever.

You will be surprised at how little the difference is. In some cases, our affordable buyers will make a greater return than on the open-market buyers.

The short explanation is that the home price is set at $450,000 as opposed to the open international market value of $1.2 million, so your property taxes are ⅓ of the open international market. Monthly mortgage payments are also ⅓.

In this new program, the down payment should be lower, with 100% financing or low-down payment programs.

To recap, we proposed protecting this market from foreign and mainland buyers. Remember, it is crucial that we have asset restrictions, residency restrictions, and resale restrictions.

Whenever I make this proposal, people say it's unconstitutional. However, it's actually similar to what our state (and almost every other state in the union) does with its affordable housing program. We also asked a constitutional expert at the University of Hawaii, and guess what? He thought it would likely be constitutional if done as part of a government affordable housing program.

I think the difference here is that we're being completely honest and upfront about creating an affordable long-term market.

This market will benefit the workers of Hawaii by keeping the home affordable for themselves, their children, and their grandchildren. One of the big problems with affordable housing now is that once the resale restriction expires (typically five to maybe 30 years) the value of the house shoots up and it is resold to someone from the mainland.

So, the solution for demand is structuring a market that gives the local buyer a chance to have all the value tied to local wages, where the price is affordable forever and the value stays among Hawaii residents. Local buyers are only allowed to buy and own one unit at a time in this affordable market for owner-occupants. They can buy and sell freely to qualified local buyers as their situation changes or they want bigger or smaller units as they go through life.

Remember, this affordable market is in addition to the present open market. We will not restrict mainland or foreign buyers, developers, contractors, or investors in the open market.

They can continue to buy and sell as they do now. They are free to compete and to buy as they see fit and as far as the laws allow.

The local market will be our affordable housing market—a government-controlled market where tax dollars are used to lower prices and concessions are given to create value for the local residents and allow them to thrive. Residents can only buy one home in the local market but are free to buy investment properties in the open market.

The difference between an open market and an affordable market is that if a homeowner in the local market sells at a higher price based on local wages, it will benefit the local buyer.

How? That's covered in the next chapter, where we will discuss balancing property taxes and ensuring everyone pays their fair share.

4

Balancing Property Taxes So That Everyone Pays Their Fair Share

The first step to correcting our market is ensuring everyone pays their fair share.

Hawaii's property tax system is fundamentally unfair because it does not recognize the difference between the variety of unit types that make up our residential real estate market.

The best example would be to imagine a subdivision where 500 homes are built. You would need miles of roadways, sidewalks, sewers, electrical, water lines, fire hydrants, street lighting, etc., all of which are paid for and maintained by taxpayers.

Now, if this were a condominium, all the cost for installing this would be included in the price of the 500 units in that single building. Further, maintenance will not be paid for by the city, but rather by the condo owners' maintenance fees.

Within the condo building, public roads in a subdivision are driveways and parking garages. Hallways are sidewalks. Streetlights are hallway lights. Sewer water and electricity are connected to one apartment after another. Piping and electrical are the responsibilities of the condominium complex.

The city does not have to maintain, repair, or upgrade the common lines in a condominium as it does in a subdivision, where it would be the city's responsibility and they would use property tax revenue to maintain them.

Moreover, if you add services like trash removal and sewer fees, you again have the cost a condominium pays in addition to property taxes. Homeowners have trash removal paid by property taxes, and condo owners pay for it directly from themselves to service providers.

Sewer fees should be lower in a condo since it maintains service lines. Unlike a subdivision, condos do not need miles of infrastructure.

The point is that condominiums and townhouses should have a much lower property tax rate, as they save the city and county money. They also save the electricity and water companies money, which should be recognized by paying lower taxes.

Also, many of our young and retired families live in condominiums, which is enough reason to cut their property taxes.

We should first reduce property taxes for condominiums and townhouses to truly reflect their cost to the city and county. The lost taxes would be made up by increasing property taxes on the single-family home. Correcting this imbalance is the first thing to do.

The second thing, assuming we've equalized the taxes between single-family and condominium, is that we need to equalize the taxes between the local owners/property taxpayers' market and off-island property taxpayers' market.

Hawaii residents are some of the highest-taxed residents in America. The one tax we all pay but forget about is sewer fees. There is no need for our high taxes other than funding government mismanagement.

A good test for taxes is a community that pays enough taxes to operate its government. However, Hawaii has additional tax revenue from visitors. Hundreds of millions in tax revenue from tourists should reduce taxes, but it does not. It just allows the government to subsidize problems rather than solve them.

We have low property taxes but high income and other taxes. Local buyers are responsible for all taxes, yet mainland buyers only pay the property taxes and taxes on income earned from rent if they declare it. To ensure all buyers are paying their fair share, I suggest we increase property taxes three-to-four times on residential properties. Once that is done, we will have enough headroom to reduce property taxes for the local buyers since they pay all the other taxes. If 30% of homes are mainland-owned, increasing property tax four-fold could generate 120% of taxes. This, I feel, would be a true reflection of fair share tax.

I would also recommend increasing the homeowner exemption on locally-owned residential property taxes anywhere from 50% to 100%. The actual reduction will depend on how much additional income is generated by the increase in property taxes for off-island property owners. You should realize that although the off-island buyers may only own 25–30% of the real estate, they tend to be the most expensive properties. It is possible that the increase in taxes on the 30% mainland-owned property could result in an increase in total property tax revenue for the county, even though local owners are paying lower taxes or no property taxes.

The main goal is that after all the adjustments, residential and apartment property owners are paying their fair share. We do not need a vacant unit tax. This one change is better and easily enforced. In this property tax proposal, the outside owners are supporting our affordable market. We now create a purpose for this market's existence.

The net result is the local taxpayer is paying less, whether this reduction in property taxes is 10%, 20%, up to 90%, or 100% for local owners. What matters is that the off-island buyers are paying their fair share, and the cost of living to the local property owners has gone down by making property taxes fair.

The taxes are reduced, and all those savings stay in Hawaii, lowering the cost of living.

Don't forget the sewer fee that was taken from the property tax and added to the water bill. It started off small, but today, it exceeds our water bill in many cases. Our politicians took advantage of us. If the politicians propose a separate fee, say no. Remember, not long ago, they suggested a garbage fee. NO, NO, NO to all these tax gimmicks.

Since we are talking taxes, the next chapter will also deal with another recommended tax change.

5

More Tax Changes: Tax the REITs

REIT stands for "Real Estate Investment Trust." It is a form of ownership where a trust company can own hundreds of millions (or billions) of dollars' worth of real estate. Individual investors who will benefit from the real estate ownership buy and sell the REIT's stock.

One of the advantages of REIT ownership is that the REIT pays no federal income tax. Because we adopted the federal tax code, mainland owners of shares in Hawaii REITs pay no Hawaii INCOME taxes.

Under federal law, REITs are required to distribute at least 90% of their taxable income to shareholders. The government then taxes the dividends "paid" as income tax. So, most REITs distribute 95% of their earnings as dividends. Only about 3% of the shareholder beneficiaries are residents of Hawaii, so about 97% avoid Hawaii income taxes.

The exemption in federal tax law actually benefits the federal government since the individual tax rate is higher than the corporate tax rate. So, this provision benefits the federal government by allowing them to collect larger amounts of federal taxes.

Realize that REITs OWN most of our hotels, major office buildings, apartment complexes, industrial parks, shopping centers, and solar farms. According to a *Civil Beat* article dated April 26th, 2019, by Roger Epstein, "REITs own about $18 billion worth of properties in Hawaii." I can assure you they own considerably more than 18 billion today. They are substantial real estate owners in Hawaii but pay no local income taxes. I would estimate their holding present value (not sales price) to be in the hundreds of billions of dollars.

For the State of Hawaii, this means we collect no taxes on REITs and lose income tax revenue. In the legislative hearings, I believe they had exhibited the Hilton

Hawaiian Hotel, the Hyatt Hotel, and Ala Moana Shopping Center, to name a few, paying no income tax on all the income they earn.

The REITs argue that the tax is a small amount of money and that changing the law would only discourage investing in Hawaii.

I don't see it that way.

Connecticut taxes REITs, and REITs continue to buy and invest in that state. They have a solid real estate market. There is no market better than Hawaii. So, if we tax them, they won't leave. And if we do, that is a good thing. A tax-paying entity will buy the property from them.

Moreover, because REITs pay no taxes, then as buyers, they can pay a higher purchasing price. It is not only unfair to local investors competing to buy assets but also paying taxes that off-island owners and REITs do not pay. It also is unfair to residents and visitors because this increases rents, which adds to our cost of living. The higher sales prices raise property taxes for all. They are distorting our market and raising our cost of living.

REITs say taxes are small and they may pull out of Hawaii. I think they're missing the point, since every taxpayer should pay their fair share.

Whether it's $1 million, $10 million, or hundreds of millions of dollars, they should pay their fair share of income taxes like all of us.

What's worse is that when they sell an asset (let's say the Ala Moana Shopping Center for $5 billion), the State of Hawaii will receive no capital gains tax under the present law. If it were privately-owned, however, the state would receive a considerable amount of tax income from the sale.

Hawaii creates enormous value in its real estate, and we require all our local companies and residents to pay taxes. Yet we give off-island owners and REITs (which are majority mainland-owned) tax-free status, increasing the cost of living to the local taxpayer.

Working with a large number of community groups and Faith Action, we succeeded in getting legislation passed in May 2019 to tax REITs. However, the Governor vetoed the bill the following fiscal year. We didn't give up and got the bill passed again—and yet again, the Governor vetoed the bill. It was at this point that one of the legislative aides asked me if we were going to finally give up or if we were going to continue getting it passed with the Governor vetoing the bill.

I mention this only because it reveals the "circus" played in our legislature. They might voice their support for a measure to be able to tell their supporters they voted in support, but behind the curtain, they're urging the Governor to veto the bill. Hawaii taxpayers should be upset and offended that our tax law allows mainland companies to do business in Hawaii tax-free. You should be insulted that your politicians permit it.

I mention this since it indirectly increases our cost of living by transferring all these mainland companies' income tax responsibilities to the taxpayers of Hawaii, which increases our cost of living. It is a sign of no commitment with all the support that the bill had; not one legislator introduced the bill again.

This is a failure of our political leadership.

6

Hawaii was a Leader in the 60s

Hawaii was a leader in building housing in the 60s. But we lost our way.

We're constantly told how it's impossible to build affordable housing in Hawaii. Yet, in 1960, we were building homes at a level that met our local market's needs. Hawaii is pretty good at building homes. In my lifetime, we have probably built over 400,000 homes. The majority of those homes (I would estimate over 50%) originally sold for under $100,000. Another 25% probably sold for under $400,000, and the last 25% sold for above $400,000. The point is, we can build affordable housing.

Our problem is that we have no mechanism for keeping housing affordable. Today, all those units will sell in the million-dollar range or more.

We always hear about the Singapore example that I used in 1985 to prove Hawaii's ability to do affordable housing. I realize now that I was misunderstood.

In the 1960s, a group of officials came from Singapore to meet with Hawaii real estate experts, attorneys, architects, and other real estate industry players.

My mother, Mary Savio, was invited to attend the meeting. Because I was fascinated with real estate, she asked for permission that I could come along and listen.

I don't remember the specific year, but it was somewhere around 1965. I recall that Singapore had become (or was going to become) a new nation, and the premier realized that the country needed to succeed. It had to solve the deplorable housing conditions that existed in Singapore at that time. It had to create wealth to fuel an economy and create good-paying jobs for its residents. They were an island surrounded by water, and their country was the size of Oahu. They did a search of countries and cities or communities that were successful at building housing for their residents. Hawaii stood out as the best example of successfully meeting the needs of its people.

Hawaii became the newest state (or 50th state) in 1959. Singapore became a new nation in the mid-1960s.

Once Hawaii became a state, our housing market boomed. We needed housing and wanted to create a strong economy so that our people could have good-paying jobs. Basically, Singapore wanted to know what we had done to make this explosion of new housing.

While I don't remember all the examples given, I do remember that we had accepted a new long-term land lease system. Prior to statehood, most of our leasehold in Hawaii was agricultural. It wasn't easy to finance residential leasehold properties. The leasehold system being used in the late 1950s was the problem. The federal government came out and asked Hawaii to modernize their land leases if they wanted to finance using FHA, VA, or any of the government programs.

Hawaii local lenders were also told they would not be allowed to sell mortgage loans to mainland institutions whose funds were guaranteed by the Federal Reserve. Basically, local lenders had to retain Hawaii mortgages on leasehold land. Hawaii was a cash-short market. We could not meet our stated housing needs if we couldn't sell loans to mainland lenders. We relied on the sale of mortgage loans to create new money that could be loaned to new local buyers.

The federal government insisted that Hawaii modernize its land lease program so that it would be acceptable to the mainland and federal regulators. All of Hawaii's lessors (except for Hawaiian Homes) adopted the modern lease, and so Hawaii's leasehold market took off. You saw new leasehold developments in Kahala, Hawaii Kai, Kailua, Ewa, Pearl City, etc. The new leasehold subdivisions opened up homeownership opportunities to most of Hawaii's residents. Housing was still a struggle, but it was doable. Families would help with the down payment. Both husband and wife had to work, but tens of thousands of local families could get into homeownership.

The other item I remember being discussed was Hawaii's adoption of a condominium statute, and it was the first state in the US to adopt condominium ownership as an alternative to single-family homes. Our condo law became the model for the entire US. Eventually, most states adopted a condo law based on Hawaii law. The condo law also allowed high-rise buildings and townhouses to be built and sold as individual units, creating further opportunities for local families to buy their first units.

The third thing I remember is discussions on the use of concrete construction—especially the use of concrete for piles. Like Hawaii, Singapore was on the ocean and needed building designs that could use piles to create stability for a high-rise building. I thought it was funny because I had only seen buildings built out of concrete all my life. It was the same old, same old for us. However, building high-rise buildings out of concrete on piles was a relatively new concept, and Hawaii was a leader in that.

Many other topics were discussed, but these are the three I remember.

The main point is that Hawaii built affordable housing in the 1960s. One of the big differences back then compared to today is that our market was still local in nature, and we had very few outside buyers putting upward pressure on our market by competing with local buyers to buy units.

The largest distortion in the 1960s was military buyers, but it was restricted to a few areas near military bases. The distortion was a few percentage points to value, at best. It was nothing like today's distortion.

Singapore adopted Hawaii's concepts, and today, Singapore is 89% on homeownership as one of the strongest economies in Asia.

They have an economy based on high-tech, banking, finance, etc. They did everything that Hawaii wanted to do using the concepts Hawaii developed. The difference is that Singapore succeeded and Hawaii lost its way, but now our people are paying the price. We are struggling.

Unfortunately, Hawaii went in the opposite direction. We lost control of our market, and our politicians lost direction. Our politicians accepted the failure and continue to build on this failure. Today, people are struggling to survive. They're being forced to leave the state because our government refuses to believe the government and our politicians are the problem.

Singapore succeeded not because of leaseholds or condominiums; they succeeded because they had a commitment to their people and realized real estate creates wealth and stability, as well as that ownership had to be held by the people, not outside investors. Singapore kept the benefits of ownership for the people—the average guy—not the wealthy.

Hawaii keeps the cost for taxpayers and gives financial benefits to the developer or wealthy owner.

Hawaii failed because the politicians told a good story but gave no commitment to the average voter. Your vote has to say, "Solve our housing crisis this term! If not, don't run again! We will not vote for you!"

Does your candidate have a solution for our housing crisis, or is it the "same old" rhetoric?

Ask them.

7

Why Do We Buy Real Estate?

Why do we buy real estate? It's not what you think, and it's not a trick question. This is just an exercise to show how much you understand real estate.

To understand the solutions to our housing crisis, it is crucial to understand why we buy real estate.

When people are asked this question, one of the major reasons they give is appreciation or an increase in value.

In reality, appreciation is wealth created, but there is a wealth creator in real estate that creates more value than appreciation. It is the real reason why you buy real estate. This wealth creator reduces or stabilizes the greatest component of our cost of living—housing.

Homeownership usually involves a mortgage you pay with a constant monthly payment. If you have a 30-year loan, your mortgage payment will stay the same for 30 years. Your income might rise over the 30 years, but your housing monthly expense remains constant.

I will use an example from 1964 to 2024 (a period of 60 years) to illustrate the difference. This is an exercise comparing renting to ownership.

In 1964, let's assume a new house sold for $25,000. Your monthly payment was $250 per month. After 30 years, your final mortgage payment would still be $250.

Your wages will definitely rise over 30 years, but your mortgage payments remain constant. Over those years, you save your pay raise and invest them as you wish. Invest in your style of living, education, saving, and/or buying more property.

To buy the home, you paid $29,000 in interest. However, your $25,000 home is worth $1 million today.

The person who rented a similar home till today started with the same $250 monthly payment. He will also get a pay raise, but his rent goes up every year as well, so his cost of living increases yearly.

The tenant will pay over $1 million in rent 60 years later. Renting is more expensive. The tenant paid rent for 60 years, but the buyer made a constant monthly payment for only 30 years.

The buyer was able to save his pay raises.

If he invested those savings, he could create $10 million in value over the next 60 years. The $10 million is an estimate of what an owner could have made if they purchased in 1960 and used savings of ownership vs. the increasing cost of rent to buy more real estate or other investments.

So, when looking at affordable housing, appreciation is not the key. The reason for buying is the constant monthly payments. If we all understand this, placing restrictions on resale price increases should not be a major concern.

Now, most people feel that resale restrictions or holding the price down on resale hurts the affordable buyer/owner, but this is not true.

The affordable owner has only two choices: rent or buy affordable with resale restrictions. If you get less appreciation due to resale restrictions on resale price, it shouldn't matter. As an owner, you have the long-term advantage of the fixed monthly payments. It allows you to keep pay raises and create wealth. You can invest the savings and create millions in value that will far exceed any benefits given up by buying into a program that does not restrict appreciation.

Also, the affordable home was cheaper, so you have even lower monthly payments. You can buy a larger or smaller unit in the local market as needed. Some appreciation is lost, but not really needed since any new unit purchased is tied to local wages. Because prices are restricted, property taxes are greatly reduced. You will receive all these savings because the open off-island market helps to support our market.

The renter created wealth but did it for the landlord. The family renting handed their family's wealth to the landlord. The landlord gets to keep the wealth. In the affordable local market, the tenant or buyer gets to keep the wealth created for themselves and their families, as there would be no landlord; just the tenant in the new local affordable market. Renting is counterproductive to the objective of living and thriving in Hawaii. That is why, in a future chapter, we will discuss why rental projects owned by an investor should not be part of any affordable housing solution. Rental buildings should be tenant-owned.

8

Reducing the Cost of Living

Any housing solution has to put housing first and must also reduce the cost of living.

In Hawaii, it is common for our legislature to come up with solid ideas. It is in the implementation phase that things go sideways. They give away any financial benefits to outsiders and lump the liabilities onto the taxpayers. Let's spend a few chapters looking at examples of good ideas being implemented poorly.

Remember, in the opening chapter, we had a quote from Milton Friedman: "One of the great mistakes is to judge policies and programs by their intentions rather than their results."

Let's look at mass transit. This is a good example of where Hawaii's leadership went wrong. Mass transit was supposed to help ease traffic congestion and ensure a cleaner environment. It was going to create construction jobs. All good reasons.

They push it through to get approval. Delays and the cost of materials increase, ballooning the cost to taxpayers. Mass transit creates 20 or more stations depending on where it will stop. Each station has about one square mile of land surrounding it that will get special high-rise zoning. This increases the value of the land.

Take Ala Moana land, for instance. It went up from $300 a square foot to over $800 a square foot. Yet the landowner gets all of that increased value for doing nothing. The taxpayers—you and me—created the value by having our taxes pay for mass transit. So, we increase our cost of living to pay for mass transit, but all the financial benefits go to the property owners.

We should charge the landowners an impact fee of $10 a square foot. This tax would raise enough to pay for and operate mass transit. Further, if the above is true, why not have an impact fee of $20 or $50 (still a small percentage of the land's appreciated value)?

Value in real estate is directly tied to density (zoning), the number of units that can be built. The size and height of the building all create value. A lot of sites increase in value automatically once zoning passes. Our city describes mass transit high-rise zoning as a ½ mile zone surrounding all 20-plus mass transit stations—basically, over 20 square miles of new high-rise zoning.

This impact fee is a tax paid by the owner to cover the impact of upzoning on his property, the community, schools, police, fire, etc. The County would assess the impact fee payable as the buildings are built.

The impact fee funds could be used to pay the cost of building mass transit and maintain its operations. This would reduce our taxes and cost of living since it is not taxpayers paying for it, but the property owners who benefited from an increase in land values. Any extra money raised could be used for affordable housing.

Under the current system, we create the value and charge Hawaii's taxpayers for the cost but give away the increased land value for free to the property owners. Our children and grandchildren will be paying for the building and operation of mass transit when it should have been free to the taxpayers and paid for by the property owners using a small part of the land value created.

Sorry, I am about to veer off-topic a little bit, but this is still part of solving the issue of what we need to do about mass transit. I say we use it to reduce our cost of living.

First, the County should set up a design team to draw a master plan for the land surrounding the stations. All the County roads should be put into the mix as developable land. We don't need the same roads in the master-planned station locations. The taxpayer owns the air rights above the road where buildings can be built. If we didn't assess impact fees, we could at least get paid for the land under the roads and parks and the air rights above them.

We should also look at the feasibility of going island-wide with mass transit. This would be done by using a mass transit bus system.

The last stop or first stop on the fixed rail Skyline system is in Kapolei. That would be the start of a mass transit bus system going to the Waianae coast.

The train would arrive and the bus would leave a few minutes later, taking the riders from the station in Kapolei to Nanakuli, Maile, and Makaha. The express buses ought to have only a handful of stops.

The leeward side riders would save on gas, conservatively saving $300 or more a month on gas by not needing to drive to and from work. A welcome reduction in the cost of living.

Our environment is improved through reducing emissions by having fewer cars on the road. The real advantage is that mass transit gets more riders from Waianae, which reduces operational losses and saves tax money, bringing our cost of living down further.

The same thing would take place at Pearl City station. As trains arrive, mass transit bus services will move people to the north shore. Let's assume there are 10 stops to go around the island and return to the Ala Moana area, or the last station on the fixed rail. We would also have buses from Kaneohe and Kailua coming into town over the Pali and Wilson tunnels. Additionally, we could have buses from Windward Side going on H-3 to Pearl Harbor mass transit station. East Oahu would have buses from Kailua side and from the last mass transit station in town.

Buses would increase the reach of mass transit to island-wide. We would have fixed the issue of low ridership on the present fixed line by extending the advantage of mass transit to rural communities. Buses would pick people up from centralized bus stations around the island and take them back to the station at the end of the workday. The key is that buses must have as few stops as possible to make travel time comparable to driving a car.

Mass transit would be available island-wide.

Remember, this is a mass transit bus system, so it should have no more than 10 or 15 stops going around the island. The travel time should be comparable to what it would take to drive.

Also, the bus mass transit system must operate efficiently to encourage ridership. Each mass transit station would act as a transportation center where smaller buses and taxis could transport passengers from the station to their desired destination within the community.

So, I've added my two cents; let's now return to the zoning matter. Even with their poor planning, mass transit created at least 20 square miles of new zoning around mass transit stations. Still, they say we need to convert our single-family districts to three units per lot. The land around mass transit will be master-planned and should handle 300,000 to 400,000 new units.

We should have a group of planners and architects looking at master planning. The UH and the public (along with other groups) should be part of a master plan to make sure units are affordable.

Vote for individuals who support thoughtful island-wide master planning.

9

Photovoltaic Program

Another case of increasing our cost of living instead of reducing it.

Let's look at another illustration where we have a great and noble idea: photovoltaic to reduce CO_2 emissions. It is a goal with strong community support, but once implemented, it adds to our cost of living and the financial benefits going to outsiders.

That, of course, is our state's photovoltaic program. Panels on the roof of houses work well, and the homeowner gets a reduction in electricity rates. There's nothing wrong with that so far—but what it really is, is a program for the wealthy because you need to own a home. Renters are left out, as are many condominium buildings, since they do not have sufficient roof space. The solution is solar farms. There are two ways to do solar farms: privately-owned or community-owned.

In Hawaii, most of our solar farms are investor/privately-owned. The electric company buys the power and charges us for the power used. However, all the money used to buy the power goes out of state. Environmentally, it reduces emissions, which is great—but financially, it has little to no benefit for the local consumer.

If all our solar farms were community-owned, all the power generated and all the money paid would reduce the cost of living by reducing or eliminating our electric bill. Community solar is similar to rooftop solar but built in large parks, with the benefits going to the renters who buy in. Instead of paying electric bills, the tenant would benefit like a homeowner. The benefits would stay in Hawaii if community-owned solar was required.

Our present model only changes how the power is generated. We used to purchase coal and oil from overseas to generate power. We then switched to solar to save the environment and no longer had to pay to buy fuel. Instead, we spent the money to buy power from solar farms (mostly mainland-owned), so the money leaves the state.

The legislature and the PUC should require that all future solar farms be owned by the community, local businesses, renters, etc.

Like the homeowners with rooftop installs, their electric bills would go down. It would reduce our cost of living, and all that money would stay in Hawaii, creating jobs, tax revenue, etc.

But we took the easy path of accepting outside ownership. We gave away the financial benefits of solar. And we get a higher cost of electricity, while our cost of living continues to increase.

We need to insist that all future solar farms are required to be locally-owned by individual renters and small businesses.

Don't forget the legislature which, using the concern over climate change, closed the power plant at Campbell Industrial Park instead of extending the contract for a few years. This plant had been reported to be generating 17% of Oahu's power needs. Existing solar was not generating enough power to replace what was lost. They used a crisis to increase our cost of living by convincing us it was needed for the environment. The local resident—the consumer struggling to survive—was thrown under the bus.

The PUC and the electric company have come up with a new program to encourage owners with solar to store power in batteries. This power could be used at night to reduce demand on the system.

This sounds good, but think about it: it is a program that favors the single-family homeowner and discriminates against condo owners and renters who do not own a home and cannot benefit from solar. It is unfair and increases the cost of living to the average resident but reduces the cost to the single-family homeowner. Yet that is what our present photovoltaic programs do. The legislature created a program that favors single-family homeowners, although it does not address condominium owners (who do not have sufficient rooftop space), nor does it address rental tenants of apartments or homes.

Again, they pushed a political goal using a crisis but increased our cost of living and fueled the forces forcing people to move to the mainland. Our legislators and political leadership's solution is to *de facto* ask us to move away. Why? Because they have no effective solutions for us despite their well-intentioned efforts. We now have brownouts because of the politicians' failure to care about the voters and our cost of living.

Every time the power goes off or we have a brownout, it isn't the electric company; it's the politicians you elected. Every time the electric bill goes up, it is not the electric company; it is the politicians you elected.

10

Rental Projects

Hawaii needs affordable rentals that benefit the taxpayers and tenant, and not wealthy building owners.

Today, I heard a political ad about how the Mayor and the Governor are working on building 18,000 rental units. Sounds great, but this could be the worst thing you can do for housing in Hawaii.

To build rental housing, we give the developers all kinds of concessions, additional zoning, financing, and tenant rent subsidies for the project's duration. It sounds good, but where is the wealth going? To the wealthy owner of the building or the non-profit.

What role does the local tenant play? He is the funnel through which all the wealth created and government subsidies flow and go to the mainland owner. In the affordable market, it actually increases the cost of housing.

This can be allowed in the international open market, as it has little to no connection to the local market.

Rental buildings are needed, but should be considered a minimal—not optimal—solution. If anything, rentals are downright counterproductive and lean into misguidance as a solution for affordable housing.

Rental units take present value and future values away from the local tenant. As costs rise and rents go up, the state will have to increase rental subsidies using our tax dollars and increasing our cost of living.

Presently, rental projects only benefit the building owner.

What is the alternative?

Well, I have it for you—tenant-owned rental buildings! This is where the building would be owned and operated to benefit the tenant. When the building's mortgage is paid off, rents go down. Thus, the tenant owner cost of living goes down, and this saves tax dollars that would have been used to subsidize rent in perpetuity.

If sold to tenants, all the funds will stay in Hawaii. The down payment to move in would be the tenant's security deposit.

The tenant would pay the same rent as if owned by an investor. We really haven't changed anything except who owns the building and who gets the benefits. In the new model, the local taxpayers/local tenants get the benefits. The taxpayers also save, so our cost of living declines.

Years ago, the city and state asked about selling their affordable buildings. I suggested selling to local developers who could convert and sell units to the tenants as a tenant-owned co-op or condo. Like an owner, they could lock in a mortgage payment for 30 years and save their pay raises. They could pay off their mortgage over time, and that portion of the total rent would be reduced. Additionally, they could save and invest money from pay increases just like an owner.

The state loved the idea and agreed to put that option in the proposal request. When the request for bids came out, it restricted tenant ownership, restricted condos, and required developers to have experience doing similar projects. They eliminated local developers and forced us to team up with mainland developers. They apologized for the misunderstanding about restricting condominiums and encouraged me to bid. But we know that if you don't follow the stated requirements, the other bidders can file a lawsuit. Behind the curtain, they structured the deal to favor mainland developers. They gave away tens of millions of dollars in potential savings and hundreds of millions in rent subsidies over the project's life—all paid by future taxes on us, the residents of Hawaii.

Again, this type of rental building is not a good idea. It keeps the cost for the taxpayers and gives the wealth away to the mainland owners.

We are not saying "Don't build rentals." We are saying "Build them smart." Do everything you are presently doing, but the ownership and financial benefits need to stay with the local renter and the Hawaii taxpayers.

The developer of a rental project should be hired as a developer for a flat fee of, say, 5%. Developers will take less risk, so they should receive a lower profit. This alone could reduce costs by 10% to 15%.

Since the project is state guaranteed, there is no need for a hefty profit as risk is reduced to the developer, and the profit should reflect that.

The state can refinance buildings once built using conventional financing, so the state guarantee is only for the construction period.

We need to let the Mayor and Governor know that rental buildings are good, but they can only really be good if the tenants or community trust own them. Rentals are only a solution if they benefit the tenant by reducing their cost of living and they are charged a set monthly rent, as a mortgage does for a homeowner.

Realize that when the government says "public-private partnership," as done today, they mean the investor (usually a mainland owner) gets the benefits, and the local taxpayers foot the bill.

Public-private partnerships can take from the state and taxpayers. It can take advantage of the tenants and use them as a funnel for the wealth to flow to the investor-owner and hand the taxpayer the liability and obligation to fund the projects' rents for life.

Investor-owned rental buildings should be avoided.

In our housing solution, a private-public partnership would have a different meaning. Where we work together, the developer builds and the public pays a guaranteed fee, but as a developer, it is risk-free or has greatly reduced risk. All the other benefits of home-ownership go to the tenant and the people of Hawaii.

It is hoped that most developer partners will be Hawaii-based, so that profits and jobs stay in Hawaii.

In short local parties, architects, contractors, engineers, doctors, and attorneys could form HUIs (i.e., Investment groups) to develop projects, much like what occurred in the 1960s. Our solution can be a strong stimulator for our business community. They are helping to solve a problem while also benefiting financially. It was done years prior, and it can be done again.

11

New Zoning

The premise here is to create new zoning to help our housing market.

We need to control the local market and protect it from investor buyers. To do this, we need to implement some new zoning classifications for our residential units. They would be:

- Residential-owner occupant only
- Apartment-owner occupant only

The title says all these lots and homes are approved and built for owner-occupants, not local or mainland investors. All new affordable units should have this restriction. We should also allow owners to put their existing homes and apartments into this program voluntarily. Most residents will give homes to their families for them to live in, effectively having it in the local market, which is a positive.

We can also allow rentals in the local and open market by structuring a program of locally-owned and rented properties in the long-term market at 100% of median income. That represents an affordable local rental since it is tied to 100% of median income. These rentals are part of (or located in) the present open market. The owner voluntarily takes it out of that market and places it in the affordable market, and its rent will be tied to local wages. This rental unit will be inexpensive, and the owner will get all the benefits of the affordable local market—especially lower property taxes.

We should also create a zoning system that allows for short-term rentals for interested investors (for instance, VRBO, Airbnb, alternate hospitality, etc.). This can be a residential or apartment zoned investor only. This is for short-term vacation rentals. This is just an example of how we increase the types of zoning to allow for particular uses for apartment investors that are engaged in long- and short-term rentals. Residential is residential; investor is investor only.

We need to do a better job of managing the competing forces for our limited housing stock and manage it to benefit our people.

I hope that many of us old-timers will be willing to put our homes and apartments into this local market program because it is what to do for our community.

Of course, by taking a home from the open market to the affordable market, we reduce your property tax, making it easier for us seniors to keep our homes till we pass them on to the next generation.

Second, if the local market reduces a unit's value, can it be considered a donation to the housing trust and create a deduction for state and federal taxes, income, capital gains, etc.? That is one of the issues we need to debate and research as we structure our affordable local housing market.

We can make a difference. We just need to believe, use a little common sense, and only vote in leaders who will lead and not just follow their party's stand and/or the whims of the "mystery power brokers" behind the curtain of Hawaii's famous "old boy" network.

12

Hawaiian Homes

It will take two-to-three years to come up with the official structure of an affordable market. This would cover all parts of the equation needed to help structure the solution.

Let's get everyone involved. Banks, appraisers, contractors, landowners, state and county governments, developers, architects, engineers, planners, unions, public representatives, carpenters, bakers, and candlestick makers.

There are three programs we can start immediately to build 30,000 to 50,000 homes. These are:

1) Hawaiian Homes

2) Section 8

3) Rental housing

Let's look at Hawaiian Homes first. It is a program that has existed for over 100 years to help Native Hawaiians become homeowners. During the first 100 years, Hawaiian Homes developed approximately 9,000 units. That's just 90 units per year.

The program has failed in its original intent and has failed in helping the Hawaiian community be successful in homeownership. Part of this is due to structural defects.

My first experience with Hawaiian Homes being structured to hold back the Hawaiian community was in the 1960s. My mother was a realtor then and had a very hard time getting Native Hawaiians to buy. There were policemen, firemen, and teachers, just to name a few professions. They had good jobs and could buy any house, but they insisted on waiting for Hawaiian Homes.

Back then, Hawaiian Homes had a rule that said if you owned a house in the open market, you could not qualify for Hawaiian Homes. So many qualified Hawaiian buyers did not buy on the open market, even though they were qualified. They decided to wait for a house under the Hawaiian Homes program. Many in this category are still renters—not owners—60 years later.

The Native Hawaiians were adamant about living and raising a family in the Hawaiian Homes communities. They realized that buying a home on the open market made sense, but they wanted to keep the right to buy in the Hawaiian Homes program.

My mother tried changing the rules but was told not to "rock the boat." She was told the rule existed to stop Native Hawaiians from maintaining wealth and power. She was reminded that the overthrow of the kingdom was not that long ago, and many people still had memories of the monarchy.

The rule that caused Hawaiians not to buy on the open market if they wanted to buy into a Hawaiian Homes community was wrong and unfair. I believe it was changed in the 70s after years of complaining. Today, Native Hawaiians can own a home in the open market and still own a home in the Hawaiian Homes program.

When my mother told us about being instructed not to rock the boat, I realized that to the Hawaiian community, Hawaiian Homes was not just about buying a home. It was more than that.

It was about protesting the overthrow of their kingdom, living together as Native Hawaiians, and preserving their language, traditions, and culture. Buying in Hawaiian Home's program was a purely pro-Hawaiian decision that is not understood today.

The federal government developed these programs for America's and Hawaii's Native peoples with the intention of failure. With statehood, Hawaii took over as trustee of the Hawaiian Homes program. You would have thought that all the wrongs done while it was a federal program would be undone. However, we still find the federal and state governments holding the Hawaiian Homes program captive today—and by extension, the Hawaiian Community.

The Hawaiian Homes program has not created wealth at the same rate as other homeownership programs. A non-Hawaiian Homes lessee who purchased in 1960 compared to a Hawaiian Home lessee who bought at the same time would realize a huge difference in value.

The non-Hawaiian leaseholder who bought a home for $25,000 in the 60s on any other leasehold land would have a home worth $1 million. That lease would also have saved another $1 million. If invested, it could have created a net worth of over $5 million.

When compared to the typical Hawaiian Homes lessee with a home purchased at $25,000 in 1960, it is probably only worth $50,000 to $100,000 now due to the age of the home and the fact that the old-style leases used by Hawaiian Homes do not allow you to value the lease. Under the old-fashioned lease, you can only value the improvements. Unfortunately, the age of houses and the value of improvements go down over time.

As a program, Hawaiian Homes will continue to fail in its mandate to help the Hawaiian community become successful through homeownership. The reason for that was mentioned earlier in this book, where we talked about how all landowners agreed to accept the new lease system in the late 1950s, allowing residential leases to be financed through all federal housing programs. All the estates accepted the new lease except for Hawaiian Homes.

It is important to understand the difference between the two leases. The Hawaiian Homes lease only allows the improvements to be valued. The leasehold value of the lease cannot be counted or used to finance Hawaiian Homes. However, this is permitted on other leases, reducing or eliminating the need for a down payment.

A Hawaiian Homes lease is better than a market lease if you only look at rent and term or length of the lease. The lease is $1 a year for 99 years.

Due to the long term of 99 years and low rent, the lease is equal to the fee simple value. When the lease is given to a Native Hawaiian family, it would have a value equal to the fee simple value of the lot.

Let's say the lot is worth $500,000. That means the Hawaiian family would need no down payment and could finance 100% of the cost of the new home since the value of the lease can be included in the appraisal. This solves the biggest problem for buyers in Hawaii, predominantly Native Hawaiians. When they get a modern lease, they are getting their down payment in the form of the appraised leasehold value.

The Hawaiian Homes low-rent, long-term lease is superior to a market lease, which has a shorter term and rents that increase over time. Hawaiian Homes leases will be extended at expiration, while market leases must be surrendered or returned to the landowner. The Hawaiian Homes lease has an advantage to the Hawaiian community. It could be restructured so that it becomes an advantage to the Native Hawaiian and to Honolulu mortgage lenders.

However, using the old form of lease takes away the value and all the advantages created by a Hawaiian Homes lease. Using the old lease may cross the threshold of incompetence to criminality, for it siphons value away that may have been used to help achieve the spirit of the program put in place for the Native Hawaiian community.

The federal government and the state risk being sued for gross mismanagement of the trust by not converting them to modern leases. It was required years ago by the federal government from all other Hawaii lessors. The loss in value to the Hawaiian community over the 100 years of the trust would be hundreds of billions of dollars.

However, the bigger losses are more challenging to quantify, as the modern lease could help the Hawaiian community finance opportunity costs lost under the old lease. Additional tremendous opportunity costs and collateral costs could have occurred such as educational opportunities, resulting in unrealized, impacted, jeopardized, or lost career paths, other real estate buying opportunities, and hosts of others. This has added impetus to leave the State of Hawaii for greater opportunities on the mainland, with the added outcome of further deterioration of the Native Hawaiian cultures.

If the new lease had been adopted, in 1959, everyone on the waiting list could have obtained a home. They could have refinanced and invested. Instead of being worthless due to age, their homes today would be worth a million dollars. They could have helped their children buy a home under the Hawaiian Homes program. The Native Hawaiians could live in Hawaii and thrive in their culture and on their land.

Basically, every Hawaiian could live and thrive in Hawaii rather than flee to the mainland. We would all be better off if this one change had gone through and been codified, so we need to tell the politicians to modernize the lease.

We have failed the Hawaiian community. For 60 years, the politicians have allowed this to happen. All around them, the politician, his family, and his friends were creating wealth with the modern lease, although Hawaiian Homes was denied the same benefit to the Native Hawaiian community by keeping the old lease.

A theft of the worst kind occurred—the near collapse of Native people, their language, and culture. Despite it all, the Hawaiians have survived, but with a considerable loss of value and potential wealth.

Like Singapore, the Native Hawaiians could be one of the wealthiest and most successful Native people in the world if they had simply been given the same opportunity as other lessees in Hawaii's acceptance of a new lease in 1959.

And we're not even mentioning the misrepresentation of the new lease system. In trying to explain why they decided not to migrate to the new system, politicians told the Hawaiian community that if their land was under the modern lease, they would have lost the land or been forced to sell it like the other estates. This is not true because it is a federal and state trust.

So, before we start solving our housing crises by building on Hawaiian Homes land, we first need to have the state modernize the lease so that it is acceptable to all federal lenders. In doing that, the 9,000 present Hawaiian Home lessees who own property have the potential to become millionaires overnight.

Those who already have houses in the Hawaiian Homes trust that need repairs would be able to borrow the money required to modernize, expand, or renovate their homes without dipping into their pockets. Native Hawaiians who want to refinance to help their children buy a home under the Hawaiian Homes program could also do that.

With a modern lease, the Native Hawaiian family would receive the land lease award and should be able to finance a house with no additional cash required, as the value of the lease could represent their down payment.

If we don't change the lease system, Hawaiian Homes will continue to fail in creating a wealthy Hawaiian community. They may build more homes, and they may generate more ownership, but Hawaiian Homes does not create value for its people because of the failure to use a modern lease. Our state is the trustee of Hawaiian Homes, and we are failing the Hawaiian community.

In the 1950s, the federal government asked all the estates to adopt a modern lease. Hawaiian Homes did not—and today, they want you to believe they cannot change the lease. They would have you believe they can only use the lease they're currently using and cannot modernize it.

To me, this is not true. They simply have to ask or advise the federal government that they are changing and amending their lease to conform to all the federal lending programs. If the federal government or the State of Hawaii trustee does not agree to the change, the Hawaiian community could sue them for billions of dollars in lost potential value. To me, it is analogous to a crime because it steals the benefit of the new lease. They are robbing opportunity from the Native people. A loss of opportunity for their wealth and future. To me, this is a gross mismanagement of the trust.

The advantage of building for Native Hawaiians immediately while the affordable housing program is being structured is that they are residents, and their income is tied to wages. The sales are restricted to only Native Hawaiians, so we can keep the investors and outside buyers out of the market. Additionally, we satisfy our obligation to the Native Hawaiian community.

So, the state should immediately modernize the lease for existing and new lessees. The existing leaseholders would have homes that go from low value to market value.

With a stroke of a pen, most current leaseholders would shift from low-value property owners to near millionaires. This sudden shift means they can now rebuild or add on. They could help their kids buy a Hawaiian Homes property, making it easier for their children and grandchildren to buy a Hawaiian Homes lease.

Our federal government has absolutely failed the Hawaiian community; over the last 60 years, the politicians have failed the Hawaiian community. It is time for our state government to right the wrongs. This move would bring Native Hawaiians home from the mainland and rightfully give them a fair place in their homeland, our state government, and our state economy.

It's essential to understand the mortgage debt is not on the land, but on the leasehold interest, and if there is a default on the loan, the lender cannot foreclose on the land in fee, but can only foreclose on the leasehold interest. Then, the lender can sell the leasehold interest to another Native Hawaiian buyer.

Once the new lease is used, Hawaiian Homes does not have to finance or guarantee the homes being built, but the buyer should be able to qualify, as any other buyer in Hawaii would qualify.

The lease should allow Hawaiian Homes to build 30,000 to 40,000 homes with little to no problem. The advantage of starting our affordable housing program by selling immediately to a Native Hawaiian is that you automatically tie the property to income here in Hawaii because the Hawaiian Homes buyer would have to live here to own the home. This works even before the land trust for affordable homes is established. Hawaiian Homes trust does what we are trying to do with our local affordable trust, where wages are tied to price.

Even though we have not established the rules for our new housing market, Hawaiian Homes is one of the programs that would automatically be covered, only allow sales to Native Hawaiians, and exclude mainland and foreign buyers.

The legislature is aware of the problem with the Hawaiian Homes form of lease but does not want to touch it because of the division within the Hawaiian community.

A true leader would go out into the community and explain the possibilities, listen, answer questions, compromise, and find a consensus within the community to move the Hawaiian people forward. Our politicians have failed.

The greatest offenders are those who are Native Hawaiian and don't want to risk the political capital and take on the work of explaining and selling our Hawaii community on coming together to find a solution—a solution that will improve Hawaiian Homes for all Native Hawaiians.

13

Section 8

Section 8 is a federal rental program where the government subsidizes rents to residents who cannot afford to pay market rents.

At least, that's what it should be, because in 1985 it was also converted to an ownership program.

I was testifying at a state hearing in the early 1980s on Section 8 and complained that it was a program for the wealthy. It used our poor as the funnel through which all the government's funding and wealth created goes to the building or unit owner.

I encouraged the legislature to look at using Section 8 not as a rental subsidy program, but rather as a chance to create affordable homeownership opportunities. If we use it as a rental program, we subsidize the tenant and his family for their whole life. If we converted it to an ownership program, we would subsidize for a maximum of 30 years. Then, the property would be paid for and there would be no need to continue with the taxpayer subsidies. And the tenant would now have a place for their family to live forever. The Section 8 tenant monthly payment, like an owner's mortgage payment, is set, and pay raises benefit the renter and his family.

The day after the hearing, Senator Mike Crozier called me and told me he was really touched by that comment about our people being used as a funnel to create wealth for building owners.

He had talked to Senator Daniel Inouye and the Senator liked the idea of converting Section 8 to an ownership program. Five years later, I received a call from Senator Crozier, who told me the program had been approved.

To this day, our state has done nothing to fund affordable housing for Section 8 recipients. In Hawaii, Section 8 pays above-market rents, so the federal funds could be used to buy properties for our residents.

In fact, instead of building Section 8 rental projects, where all the money again flows to the wealthy owner, we should be building Section 8 ownership projects where the ownership stays and value remains with the tenants in Hawaii. The federal subsidies would stop after 15 to 30 years since the mortgage is paid off.

The fact is that we had an opportunity to help thousands of people move into homeownership using federal funds. Still, our city and state have done nothing to create or take advantage of this ownership opportunity. Think about Hawaiian Homes; every Hawaiian receiving Section 8 could become a possible buyer.

While talking to a legislator years ago, he tried to explain to me how supporting this type of program to help Section 8 tenants was difficult because how would they explain to everyone else that people on Section 8 can buy homes, but the rest of them can't be allowed to buy?

Of course, my response was, "Let's make a commitment to everyone to come up with programs to help everyone in our community become a homeowner." He wasn't impressed. This comment exhibits a lack of commitment on the part of the legislature. We look at the housing problem as individual groups with different needs and problems. We need housing programs to address all the various groups.

Section 8 is the easiest one to start with because it's a federal program using federal funds, that is paying above-market rents in Hawaii, which makes it easier to buy an affordable home in our new local market.

It's a program that both state and county housing officials should be using to place people into homeownership. If they team the Section 8 program up with Federal Farm loan programs, they will find it relatively easy to have Section 8 tenants qualify for property in our rural communities.

The federal government would guarantee the Section 8 monthly payments, and the farmers' home loan program would provide lower interest rates. Combining the two would make housing affordable for tens of thousands of families on all our islands. This is a program we should study and work on to start moving our people into homeownership.

14

Rental Buildings

The third way to immediately create affordable housing is using rental buildings. Our Governor and Mayor recently announced that over 18,000 rental units were being planned. My guess is they are not looking at rental units that would be owned by the tenants, but rather owned by wealthy off-island investors. These off-island owners would get all the benefits of ownership at the expense of Hawaii's taxpayers where incomes in Hawaii are low and rents are high.

If our government is going to give concessions to subsidize rents, grants to help with the construction, maybe subsidize interest rates for the developer, waive development fees, etc., it will all remain the same. The one thing that would change in the rental program is who owns the building and gets the financial benefits. Simply requiring all buildings to be locally-owned by a tenant association would set us on the way to solving our housing crisis.

The state may have to fund the equity and work with the present developer, and hopefully convert them to a developer-for-fee arrangement. Under this agreement, the developers agree to make a substantially lower profit but take no risk in return for the development of the property.

The state would be responsible for the equity, all loan guarantees, and all funding. In doing this, we get the benefits of qualified and experienced developers. They are compensated fairly for the time they spend building the project risk-free. Basically, the developer becomes the construction manager of the project, and since they're at a lower risk, they could take on more projects and develop rental units or owner-occupant homes even faster.

By reducing the developer's profit to a flat fee, we are also reducing the price of the units by at least 5% to 10% or more. Ownership of rental projects makes a lot of sense for Hawaii and gives our tenants the benefits of ownership in terms of stability. They would have an excellent place to live, and having a fixed monthly payment means they can create wealth as their income rises over time. Also, their rents rise at a much lower rate, so they don't face large rent increases and can start saving money.

This concept would create the opportunity for tens of thousands of tenants to move into buildings they would own in the future. As tenants/owners, they would have most of the rights of ownership in terms of a place to live with stable monthly payments.

At some point in the future, the loan on the building would be reduced and the rent would be lowered accordingly. We talk a good story about wanting to help our people stay in Hawaii and live a good life, but every rental and affordable program we presently have simply uses our people as a funnel through which the wealth will flow to the building owner.

The state and county housing directors must understand that ownership creates wealth while renting takes that wealth from the tenants. To me, rental buildings are counterproductive to the goal. They should only be used in a temporary situation while you're waiting to save and move into your tenant-owned building or another property to be developed. We need to change our concept on rentals and the building of all future rental projects as tenant-owned.

This is not a big change; we're going to do exactly what we're doing to develop rental buildings now. The only thing we're asking to change is who will end up owning the building. Remember, the real estate owner gets all the value and success that comes from ownership. We need the equivalent of rental buildings, but all future buildings in Hawaii should be tenant-owned rental projects where the people of Hawaii own the buildings in some form of trust.

The tenants are treated like property owners and get the benefits of ownership in terms of a fixed monthly payment. After 30 years, their mortgage would be paid off and the rent would be eliminated. Just like the monthly payment that comes with homeownership, the tenants in tenant-owned buildings are creating wealth for their families and for our community.

15

Rent to Build Equity

This is one of many variations that could be used to get locals into homeownership. In this case, the program is for tenants who cannot qualify for a loan or a Section 8, as they cannot purchase due to extenuating circumstances. Rent to build equity would help them continue renting, but it would be in a program that creates value for them.

This is a similar situation where the building could be investor-owned, but the tenant builds equity. The investor/owner may get some of the benefits, such as depreciation and tax savings. Homeowners/buyers do not have access to depreciation provisions and tax savings. Giving that to the buildings or units' investor/landlord/owner could reduce the tenants' rent, making the unit more affordable or the rent held at the market rate.

A larger monthly amount will go to the buyer's equity buildup, becoming their down payment. Once the buyer has overcome the problem that stopped them from being able to buy or qualify for a loan, they can take the equity and buy another unit. This is about commitment. Every program we discuss may have variations to help every renter become a homeowner. This type of total commitment is what we need to get all our people into the stability of homeownership.

The simple, easy-to-explain single "solution" used over the last 60 years will fail. We need a complete program where everything is about local ownership and wealth creation for all our residents. There is no way to outline all the possibilities, so I am using the rental program as an example of how we can amend the program. It keeps the concept of benefiting the tenant.

We're not asking to create some elaborate program; all we're asking is to change who will own the rental buildings. We are planning to build and subsidize the units in numerous ways to benefit our tenants and turn them into property owners. Why not keep the wealth for our community? It should be a relatively straightforward program that could be implemented immediately.

The many possible tweaks only open the program to more potential tenants wanting to become buyers.

16

What Would an Ownership Program Look Like in Hawaii?

The first thing we would need is a statewide agency responsible for administering all the various programs tasked with creating a local affordable housing market and its related programs.

These would be programs for the developer, the lenders, the attorneys, the buyers, etc., to ensure we are working together to create affordable housing.

It's important to remember that the first part is about creating and building ownership and rental properties. They must be affordable for our people. We need to develop programs that will allow them to buy, finance, and live in these projects.

The second part is how we establish programs to maintain the affordability of these units into the future and make sure the pricing will always be affordable for our people.

We've already covered three opportunities to create affordable housing while our community figures out what laws and regulations are needed to implement statewide housing programs. I assume it would take three-to-four years of discussion among our legislature, bankers, developers, and the community to arrive at an acceptable format or entity for managing and maintaining the affordable housing program.

We may want to look at Singapore in terms of how they handled and master-planned their housing development. We have existing entities that could easily take over the responsibilities of a state housing initiative.

This is where all ownership restrictions need to be embedded in its documentation.

The restrictions required to enter the affordable market have already been discussed:

- A resident of Hawaii
- Cannot own other real estate
- Income and asset restrictions
- Any other affordable requirements we decide would be necessary
- Appreciation tied to wages

The requirements to enter the market are needed right away so that we can start building affordable housing immediately.

We've already outlined the three markets we can build immediately for:

- Hawaiian Homes
- Section 8
- Tenant-owned rental buildings

All three are tied to local incomes and other restrictions. We have already discussed being a resident, income restrictions, asset restrictions, buyers' age, owning no other property, etc., so we could add other restrictions to ensure the market only caters to residents and workers.

The first thing to consider in the three markets is how developers are compensated. As a rule, developers have to put up large amounts of assets and personally guarantee the development loan. Because of the risk they take, they can make profits in the 15% to 20% range. For the risk they take, it is a fair return. In fact, banks are hesitant to finance projects where developers don't have enough cash and/or contingencies to structure the development.

In the new market, the first thing we should do is eliminate the developers' risk, and in return, they accept a lower profit (let's assume 5%), which means we save 10% to 15% off the buying price.

We will discuss how the developers' risk is reduced, but the simple explanation is that the developer will not guarantee the financial side of the project.

The easiest way to accomplish this is to have a schedule of fees paid to developers for putting the project together and managing the construction. This concept is known as a "developer-for-fee," with fees typically between 1% and 5%. Smaller projects attract a 5% fee, but larger projects could go down to a low fee of 1%.

I believe developers-for-fee makes the most sense. Developers take none of the risks and don't have to invest funds or guarantee a loan. They are hired to build specific projects for this program.

This would give us the expertise of Hawaii's, mainland, and foreign developers. We take on all the risk, which translates to a lower developer profit, lower prices, and lower rents.

And that is just one saving. As we go through the whole program, there will be additional savings, reducing the price even further.

We should also look at how the projects would be financed while being developed and how we will handle financing once completed because financing the developer and financing buyers can reduce the price even further.

Financing after project completion is often overlooked, but it can be a game-changer. For example, assume you have a $500,000 loan at 9% interest for 30 years. The monthly payment would just be over $4,000. However, at:

- 6% – That same mortgage payment would be just under $3,000.

- 5% – Monthly payment would be just under $2,700.

- 3% – Monthly payment would be $2,100.

So, reducing the interest rate alone could lower the monthly payments from $4,000 to $2,100 for a $500,000 home.

For the developer, construction loan payments without interest could mean huge savings and cost reduction. The savings in interest could mean another 5–10% in price reduction annually.

For the buyer, the savings realized from reducing the interest could decrease the monthly mortgage payment considerably, making the unit more affordable.

It's important to realize that PRICE is a major consideration, but the interest rate also has a huge impact on monthly payments. Any structure or plan for housing should take into consideration price and interest rate. We should also remember that steady/constant monthly mortgage payments are critical to creating wealth and stability for a buyer.

We often concentrate on price and lose sight of all the other aspects of real estate: wealth creation, debt, etc. It's the interaction of all these parts that have to be structured to create an affordable alternative for our local market. I don't know what the final structure will look like, but I do know it will need to contain almost everything discussed in this book. We need to determine how to structure the needed interest rate program to keep payments affordable. We must ensure we include it in a coherent housing policy for our state.

Remember, we are keeping the existing market: the international or open market where the developers, the banks, and everyone can do what they've always been doing. We are not going to take away anything from that market.

What we are doing is creating a whole new market that will build affordable housing for our people. It is in this market that all the regulations, concepts, programs, etc. will work to create affordability.

Remember, present developers can do what they have always done. They can also add affordable projects if they like the new program.

Additionally, architects, contractors, and others can put together teams to build in the affordable market. The market is structured to attract new developers willing to enter the market knowing that profit will be limited, but so will the risk and the need for cash. The whole purpose of everything we do is to create affordable housing.

I am hoping Hawaii's present developers may open affordable housing divisions that will do affordable housing under this new program. I explained my program to a developer friend and was surprised by his support. He also demonstrated his willingness to open an affordable division and do affordable development under this program.

This new local market must be regulated primarily to stop outside investors, retirees, etc. from buying the affordable units.

We need a structure that will keep the units affordable to local buyers forever. I still strongly believe in tying future prices to increases in local wages/income. This would be the most straightforward way to control future prices. Basically, that is how our market would work if we had no outside buyers distorting Hawaii's market. Remember, the definition of a local real estate market is where prices are tied to wages.

I believe in what we have outlined in this book and the concepts needed to move forward with a successful plan to build housing for our people.

It looks complex, and it probably is. The devil is in the details, as it is often said—but at the same time, I believe it's relatively straightforward. Individual programs are easily structured. The total concept of a market for local residences that will hold hundreds of thousands of units is where we have to spend the time and effort to structure and establish a system that will make housing available for our residents.

We were on the road to success in the 1960s, but we have lost our way. Singapore took our concept, kept its eye on the target, and succeeded. We can do the same thing now and catch up to them.

We're 60 years behind, but within 30 years, we should be able to catch up with Singapore and other states and countries that are running successful affordable housing programs. A majority of our people would then own a unit, and those who have moved to the mainland would be able to return.

I think the message to everyone is that you have to believe it can be done and accept that we have failed for the last 60 years, and it's nobody's fault. It's a fact, and we have to try an alternative solution.

17

Legislative Action – A Complete Housing Program

The first and most important thing we need to do is understand the problem and support the solution.

We need commitment and a complete housing program. Currently, we have no real commitment or complete program. All we have are bits and pieces: new rental projects here, developing the stadium area there, etc. New rental projects are not a program. Where is the plan to reduce price, reduce the monthly payment, and encourage development on a massive scale? We need a commitment to Hawaii voters; to house our people, it needs to be a complete housing program. We also need a commitment to put people first, not a political party.

For any new program to be completed, it must include a clear understanding that we have a DEMAND problem, NOT a SUPPLY problem. Once this is accepted, then we need to:

i. Split our market into two separate markets.

ii. Keep our present international market open to everyone. Here, new units will be built, sold, and resold in an open market. There will be no restriction on the price in the open market. Therefore, properties can be sold at what the market can attract. It is no different from the open market we presently have in Hawaii.

iii. Establish a new local market that will be created and built under a government housing trust. Units will be kept affordable forever by restricting appreciation and resale prices tied to wages, which increase gradually. The units can be sold simply with a deed restriction or a land lease with rent and prices tied to wages. Land rents will also be affordable. The leasehold system is structured to benefit the homeowner, not the landowner. Leases can be extended or, if canceled/expired, replaced with a newer unit for the leases. In our local market, we are committed to keeping our people housed.

While the legislation is being prepared to set up the public trust, we should start with five affordable markets/programs:

1) For Section 8 renters who wish to buy. The government will help with a down payment and provide a framework for qualification.
2) Hawaiian Homes. The state will push more Hawaiian Homes onto the market and help all Native Hawaiians own homes. This brings the need to modernize existing and new leases to the forefront. Homes could also be fee simple but have deed restrictions that would be in a modern Hawaiian Homes lease. Property can only be sold to Native Hawaiians.
3) Rental projects. These will be built as they are currently but owned by the tenants, not an investor. The intention is to transfer these buildings to the public trust once completed. The

rent increase for the mortgage portion will be based on a fixed monthly payment with no increases. Maintenance fees can be raised. Tenant associations will hire firms to manage the rental building using a condo association management company.

4) For affordable units, all affordable units built by developers in the open market will also be conveyed to the public trust once established.

5) For existing property placed into the affordable market, developers and owners who want to place properties they own into the affordable market can. The advantage is that the price at which the property is put in will be the basis for property taxes. Price cannot be greater than the median income (100%) can afford to pay. It is assumed that these are owners who will hand over the property to someone in their family and/or want to do their share of keeping housing affordable for Hawaii's people. If possible, we should structure the program so that donations at a lower price create a tax deduction for the value of the amount donated to the community. It could take the form of a reduction in

value or a price reduction—something a tax expert can figure out.

While we are establishing public trust, we must work on the finance programs needed by developers and buyers. These first three programs should try and use federal funds, such as Section 8 rental assistance and farmer's home loan program with its low-interest rate programs for those willing to buy in rural areas. On Oahu, that could be units on leased parts of Ewa, Central Oahu, North Shore, etc.

A. We need 100% financing for developers. They take no risk and reduce profits to a percentage of sales price—let's assume a max of 5%. On a $40 million project, a developer would earn a fee of $2 million at 5% for a project he puts together, and they would manage the development for, say, two years. The developer earns less but also takes less risk and should be able to manage more than one project. It also means developers in the open market may set up divisions to manage and build projects in the affordable market.

The state can guarantee the loans using mortgage insurance, where the only guarantee the developers need is the equity portion, similar to how the top 10% to 20% of a 100% mortgage is covered by insurance. The state only has to insure the equity piece. We only need to work with lenders to determine what that would be.

This could also take the form of a Hula Mae program for developers, where low-interest rate bonds are sold and the funds from the bond sale are loaned to developers to build affordable homes and condos.

The low-interest rate financing and funding of the equity could reduce prices by another 10% due to the savings under the program.

> **B.** We will also need financing for the buyers, which will allow for zero/no money down payment financing or:
>
> - Down payment loans at low interest rates; or
> - Grants so that they can finance with little or no cash

Remember, our renters live paycheck to paycheck. It's not their fault, but the government's fault for allowing our housing crisis to continue unchecked for 60 years.

The lower the buyer's income, the lower the interest charged on the buyer's mortgage. Lower interest rates lower the monthly payment. We can't control the price of the components that go into a house, but we can subsidize interest rates, making units more affordable.

Most of these ideas were developed when I was a student at the University of Hawaii majoring in real estate. We could have solved the problem, but our government lost its way and its commitment to the people of Hawaii.

 C. We need to work with the unions on allowing manufactured housing in and out of state. We need to ensure our local trade unions support the program and support them to be assured that Hawaii will always have skilled workers on the island. Remember, we are isolated, so we must make sure all aspects of our community are strong. This means we need to support both unions and non-union companies and workers.

We should look at manufactured homes built in Hawaii or brought into Hawaii and ensure they can only be used in the local affordable market. They will also be subject to the future value being tied to wages. Remember that each buyer is creating wealth, and all that wealth is staying in Hawaii. Buying the home may result in payments that are lower than what the buyers are presently repaying as rent, which reduces their cost of living. If you buy an affordable unit, you are locking in your highest monthly cost of living (rent) for 30 years by buying a home.

The manufactured home, if purchased at 100% of the median income or less, will be sold at that income level and always resold at that income level. We should be able to get homes priced at less than 100% of median income. Working with the government, unions, and banks, we should (with subsidies and creative financing) get homes for all wage earners in Hawaii.

> **D.** Union and non-union contractors are needed to do affordable housing. We need to attract and train more carpenters and workers in general and bring back the workers that left.

E. We should investigate whether a program structured for affordable housing could generate federal and state tax refunds, if price reductions are considered tax-deductible contributions to the non-profit running the local market trust. This may encourage owners to put existing residential properties into the local market.

F. Prices in an affordable market should be tied to wages. This results in keeping units affordable forever. This is basically the definition of a local market without any outside distortion.

Restrictions to Keep Market Local and Available for First-Time Buyers

In the local market, appreciation is controlled by wages. This means the market will forever be affordable for local buyers. Once you enter the market, you can trade freely within as your family grows or your needs change. The market protects you from price influence by off-island wealth and allows you to create wealth for your family and community.

FIRST-TIME BUYERS

I would define a first-time buyer as someone who has not owned a real estate property for the last five years. This would allow people who sold or were foreclosed on a chance to buy in.

RESIDENT OF HAWAII

Under this program, residents should be defined as individuals who have lived in Hawaii for at least five years. Most local families make this cut easily, and it is not restrictive for new buyers. If it is too restrictive, then buyers are required to have worked and received wages on the island for at least one-to-three years. Remember, we restrict appreciation; we restrict assets to enter the market. So, there are parts of the program that act as a mechanism to restrict the affluent buyer. This is to further establish and solidify the LOCAL market.

NET WORTH

Buyers entering the local market cannot have a net worth of more than $200,000. The combination of all the restrictive requirements ensures we are assisting the buyers who really need the help. This is important, as it will restrict more affluent purchasers who can buy without government aid. They can buy in the open market.

RESIDENTS MUST BE HAWAII TAXPAYERS

The buyer should be a Hawaii taxpayer, have resided in Hawaii for at least a year, and have filed income taxes with the state showing employment income for 12 months.

INCOME RESTRICTIONS

It can be the present median income used for affordable housing (100%) or even less.

REAL ESTATE EDUCATION

All buyers must take classes in real estate, so they are prepared to buy and budget and be successful in homeownership.

COUNSELING PROGRAM

We need to educate our workers on homeownership but also have coinciding support if a problem comes up. This would be for buyers who have problems with death, illness, a lost job, etc. There will be buyers who need help, and we will need funds available to offer such temporary help.

The list can be expanded as time goes by to make the program work. Problems or issues that arise could be added by the trustees of the soon-to-be-established housing trust.

The point is that if we work together and for the people, we can do this. We can make housing affordable. We can keep our families in Hawaii and we can bring our families home. We can fulfill Prince Kuhio's dream of housing for the Native Hawaiian community and fulfill our stated commitment to the Native Hawaiian community and all our residents. We should be entitled to an affordable unit for us and our families.

18

Changes in Government

Our present legislative process allows for the system to be overwhelmed, and according to a few legislators and lobbyists, every legislative session is a rushed affair. The people's voice is left out or greatly restricted in the present process. Yes, I am painfully aware that the rules of the legislature are out of my area of expertise, but I know they are structured in such a way as to discourage public engagement.

We need a more open legislature—to go to a full-time legislature. It will cost more, but the money, pain, and waste of our tax dollars under the present system all say we need a change. I would suggest extending the legislature to a year-long process.

It would look something like what I outline below:

All bills are introduced in the first two weeks of January. This would slow things down and give the public a chance to review, study, and respond.

Hearings are scheduled for February through April. A minimum of a one-week notice is given for hearings, and if changed, another one-week notice is given.

The first vote on proposed bills will be in May.

Whatever the balance of days in May combined with June will be used to study changes and amendments that were passed.

In July, we will start the second half of the legislative session. We have hearings in July and August.

In September, bills that survive have 30 days to be sent to the committee to change and reach an agreement.

In October, bills are passed for the Governor to sign.

I am no expert on the process, but the point is that the chaos and mad rush we have at each leg of the legislature keep the public away and let the "old boy" network control and manipulate the process. The present structure is not inviting to the public and discourages participation.

We need more time and a process where the public can speak up and think about what is proposed.

I would rather pay for an extended session than pay for another 60 years of failure.

19

Send a Message to the Legislature

Register as a voter and vote—but also use your vote to send a message.

To make any progress in creating affordable housing, there are several things that Hawaii's residents must do:

1) Register to vote. You can't join the protest unless you are registered to vote. So do it.

2) Now that you've registered to vote, you need to actually go out and vote. Registering to vote and voting has always been low in Hawaii. Out

of those registered to vote, many do not do so. It's crucial in every election that everyone eligible to vote is registered to vote and does vote, even if with a blank ballot.

3) Use this election and your vote as a polite way to let the legislator or person running for office know how you feel. If the person is running but unopposed, vote for him if you absolutely believe he's doing an excellent job. If you have doubts, do not vote for them. Let that individual realize that people are not happy with what they are doing. They will see 10,000 ballots taken and that only 2,000 voted for them.

It's important that if 10,000 people vote and the candidate only gets 2,000 votes, they will know they need to change. They have to solve our housing crisis or we will throw them out of office.

If someone's running opposed, you need to make a choice: should you vote for the other candidate or the one who presently holds the office? Before voting for the person currently in office, ask yourself if they are worth your vote. Have they done a good job in representing us?

If the answer is yes, then vote for him, but if no, analyze the other candidate(s) and decide whether they offer a better alternative. If not, don't vote in that race.

Voting for no one is a powerful vote in itself. Taking a ballot and voting, and not voting but returning the ballot, is the key. Showing up to vote is a statement, showing up and taking a ballot is an additional statement, and not voting for candidates you don't believe in is a strong cry for help. It is a cry for a need to change. It is a rejection the candidate will see. However, the candidate will only see it if you vote and return your ballot without casting a vote for those not doing their job.

In the past, we showed up and voted—and even if running unopposed, we checked the box. I'm not sure why we voted for that candidate, other than there was no other alternative to checking the box. What we need to do is ask: "What has this candidate done to solve our housing crisis? Has he taken the lead, were they productive and taking action? Or is he just sitting back like everyone else and doing nothing?"

Let's assume that when the election results come out, maybe 12,000 people voted in the district. Still, the politician running unopposed has only received 999 votes. That's a definite indication that he would've lost the race if there had been opposition. This is the message we need to send. We, the voters, are not happy. I'm hoping that in a few elections, the candidate running with an opposition candidate would be a better alternative than the incumbent who failed to do anything meaningful about housing.

Now is the time to force a change. Remember, this will only work if people register to vote and then actually vote. Do not cast votes for candidates simply because they are running unopposed. We should never vote for someone just because they are the only name on the ballot. The key is not just to vote for the office holder if a viable alternative exists.

We need to let the politicians know we are not happy with them. Not registering tells them you are not a threat to them. You don't vote. Registering and not voting tells them not to worry since you do not vote.

But if you take the time to vote in person or mail in a ballot (even if it is a protest vote), you are now a threat because you are willing to have your voice heard. It may be a cry for help rather than a voice of support, but Hawaii has a lot to cry about. Please vote in some form.

So, *vote*. Become a threat and use your vote to send a strong message demanding a solution to our housing crisis.

20

Steps to Success

We talked about the 18-wheeler earlier in our story. We also spoke about Singapore. Let's take another look at Singapore and see how they're doing on the housing highway.

Their 18-wheeler is speeding along at 80 miles an hour. Its load is a prosperous economy, an affordable cost of living, affordable units for their people, better education—grade school through college—creating a strong economy and high-paying jobs in finance technology, banking, etc.

By managing their housing market, they have created wealth for their nation-state and for their people.

They learned from Hawaii, taking a few concepts and applying them to their economy, creating success.

Hawaii needs to do the same thing. Our leaders say we can't do what Singapore did because their market is different from ours. Hawaii must take the concept of affordable housing and create a market that will work for us.

It is not just about affordable units; it's about an economy that treats everyone fairly and creates wealth for everyone. It creates a home for your family. It's an affordable cost of living for everyone, employment and jobs for your children, and many social amenities. Our leaders have made so many mistakes and mismanaged and neglected our 18-wheeler.

I described how our 18-wheeler has 18 flat tires and how the Governor and the Mayor have filled one or two tires. The legislature filled a tire that had a leak with the three houses on one lot.

This is obviously the mistake Hawaii constantly makes. We believe we are one or two quick solutions away from the 60-year problem being corrected. We have not even started the race, and our tires are flat.

You would think we'd realize that is not the case. The 18-wheeler is the truck or the program that carries us to success, but only if we put our house in order. If we succeed, our vision will consist of affordable units, better-paying jobs, a lower cost of living, employment in plenty, higher education for all... in effect, a better place to live and a better place to raise your children.

So, let's scrutinize Hawaii's 18-wheeler. We know all the tires are flat, and our engine is broken. The engine is a critical part of our success. The engine has to be the commitment from our government as well as the commitment of our people and our voters to demand that our elected officials work on a program—a complete housing program that will bring us success. There's to be no forgiveness and no excuses—we have waited too long, and we cannot afford to wait any longer.

We need our government to develop a comprehensive housing program where all 18 wheels are full of air and ready to race down the highway to our housing success. It's important to understand that the concept is about benefiting the people of Hawaii and not the politicians, the large corporations, the banks, or the

Democratic Party. We must fill the tires on our 18-wheeler with the right programs to get us to success.

Remember, the engine is our commitment from politicians—commitment and the understanding that there's no excuse. We cannot wait. It is impossible to overstress the importance of this commitment on our politicians' part.

I cannot stress the commitment of our voters and where you vote on this one issue enough. I don't care how good the politician is at everything else; if they're not getting the housing job done, they need to step aside.

If we want to be as successful as Singapore, we want our children to be able to buy and live comfortably in Hawaii and have access to high-paying jobs and good education. It starts with the voters demanding commitment from their leaders.

Let's discuss how the tires for our 18-wheeler are going to be properly inflated.

1st TIRE – DECLARE A HOUSING EMERGENCY

The Governor and County Mayors need to declare a housing emergency, recognizing that it is a DEMAND problem, taking responsibility, and solving the housing crisis.

2nd TIRE – BIFURCATE OUR HOUSING MARKET

Keep the present international market, but it will now support and benefit the local market. Mainland and island owners (as well as investors) will pay their fair share of taxes.

Create a local market where affordable units can be purchased and sold freely to qualified residents. Rental and buying prices will be tied to local wages. These properties will remain affordable forever.

3rd TIRE – LEGISLATURE, WORKING WITH THE COMMUNITY, MUST STRUCTURE AN AFFORDABLE HOUSING PROGRAM

Appoint or create a new government agency that will oversee the approval of affordable projects and their development. This entity will enforce all the requirements to enter the new local market.

4TH TIRE – REDUCE COST OF LIVING

Ensure our local governance does not continue giving away the financial benefits while retaining the cost. Rather, the objective is to keep the financial benefits for the people of Hawaii.

5TH TIRE – MASTER-PLAN TRANSIT ZONES AROUND EACH MASS TRANSIT STATION

The communities should be involved to be assured that affordable units are built and market units pay their fair share to Hawaii's taxpayers. City and state should include all streets and roads as developable land within transit zones. As sold to developers, these funds go to affordable housing. Impact fees are charged to owners, where state-funded projects create value to the landowners at the taxpayers' expense. This mitigates this so the taxpayers' increased expense is offset appropriately.

6TH TIRE – APPOINT HOUSING ADVOCATES

The State and County Mayors should appoint housing advocates who will work together to ensure housing needs on each island are met.

7TH TIRE – CREATE FEE STRUCTURE BASED ON DEVELOPMENT COST THAT DEVELOPERS WILL RECEIVE

We remove the risk, so developers should get a lower fee for planning and building (I would think 5% or less, depending on the project's value). Developers will receive a bigger percentage for smaller projects and a smaller percentage for larger projects.

8th TIRE – VALUE CREATED STAYS IN HAWAII

All government decisions should ensure the financial benefits and value created by government decisions and programs stay in Hawaii. We must stop the cycle of residents paying for properties but benefits going to the mainland or investors.

No more social and environmental benefits to taxpayers along with its costs, with all financial benefits going to the off-island developer or builder. This ought to end.

9TH TIRE – PROPERTY TAX REFORM

Everyone must pay their fair share.

Balance property taxes between single-family and multifamily buildings (apartments, co-ops, and condos). Then, the taxes are balanced between local owners, who pay all taxes, and mainland owners, who primarily only pay property taxes. Everyone should pay their fair share. The expected increase in tax revenue should reduce property taxes on locally-owned real estate.

10TH TIRE – TAX REITs

REITs should pay income and capital gains taxes just as local taxpayers do. Everyone should pay their fair share.

11TH TIRE – PHOTOVOLTAIC PROGRAM

All new solar farms should be built by developers for a fee under the community solar program and sold to residents under a condo or co-op structure. This will reduce electric costs and provide tenants and condo owners with the same opportunities that are only presently available to single-family homeowners.

12TH TIRE – RENTAL PROJECTS LOCALLY OWNED

Continue as we currently are, but ownership, income, and appreciation stay in Hawaii, creating benefits and wealth while also reducing the cost of living for the people of Hawaii. This is a program we can start immediately.

13TH TIRE – DEVELOP HAWAIIAN HOMES LANDS

This can be done immediately, but we must stop using the archaic lease presently used by Hawaiian Homes and instead use the modern Hawaii land lease utilized by other Native land trusts and private landowners.

The new lease system gives Native Hawaiians the same benefits and creates wealth as it did for the rest of our community in the 1960s. The state, as trustee, should talk to the Native Hawaiian community about reducing blood quantum. It is fair for the tens of thousands of Hawaiians who were never offered a lease and died while waiting. This took away their children's chance to be granted a lease.

14TH TIRE – BUILD UNDER SECTION 8 OWNERSHIP PROGRAM

Set up a program to help Section 8 tenants buy real estate. We can start immediately by using federal money. The biggest need is down payment loans or grants. Additionally, a course of classes on real estate and budgeting ought to be required.

15TH TIRE – NEED UNIONS' SUPPORT

Unions need to support packaged or factory-built homes with the understanding that they can only be used in the affordable market, and not the international market. We should all support building factories in Hawaii to build these homes.

We need 50,000 homes right now, but we could use another 50,000 for those who have left and want to come home. This should create jobs for union and non-union workers.

16ᵀᴴ TIRE – NEED TO EDUCATE RESIDENTS AND BUYERS

Our schools need to teach about real estate, renting and owning, and its importance to our people and the economy.

17ᵀᴴ TIRE – DEVELOP GOVERNMENT FINANCING PROGRAMS

We need special financing programs to help developers, renters, and buyers. Various programs are needed to facilitate favorable interest rates and low down payments. Reducing interest rates is the easiest way to make housing affordable.

The government does not need cash, but could structure programs using insurance, similar to what FHA and VA programs offer.

18ᵀᴴ TIRE – HOMES IN THE LOCAL MARKET BE PRICED AND TIED TO LOCAL WAGES

Base affordable prices for homes and apartments on local wages. The price is not tied to what outside buyers will pay, but rather to what the local community can pay. The homes and apartments in this program shall remain affordable, forever.

SPARE TIRE – DEVELOP NEW ZONING

- Owner Occupants Residential ONLY
- Investor Owner Residential ONLY (may be long- or short-term)

To close, I feel it is appropriate that we end with the first quote we began with by Milton Friedman:

> *"One of the great mistakes is to judge policies and programs by their intentions rather than their results."*

In summary: if we work together, it is possible to make our desired outcome achievable.

Acknowledgments

If you have made it this far, thank you for taking the journey with me. I hope this compendium (or perhaps compilation) of takes on a variety of topics regarding housing and our government policy has been inspiring and helped reframe the problem in your mind.

I also want to give a SPECIAL THANKS to the following people, whose efforts have made this entire work possible.

- My Wife and Family, for their unending support.
- Pavel Stanishev, my Layout and Format Designer.
- My Chief Contributor, Jameson Dahl; without his efforts, this project wouldn't have happened.
- The Zippy's Breakfast Club: of my Accountant & Developer Team, who have met once a month for over a year searching for solutions.

About the Author

Peter Savio is a seasoned real estate developer and visionary entrepreneur with extensive experience in property investment and development.

Born in Hilo, raised in Hawaii, and serving as the Founder and President of Savio Realty Ltd., he has played a pivotal role in shaping the real estate landscape in Hawaii.

When is he not actively working on real estate projects. He enjoys spending his "off" time with his family or in his garden. He hopes you have enjoyed this book, and says Mahalo for taking the journey!

www.ingramcontent.com/pod-product-compliance
Lightning Source LLC
Chambersburg PA
CBHW052255220526
45471CB00001B/353